MUCH ADO ABOUT NOTHING

MUCH ADO ABOUT NOTHING

William Shakespeare

Edited by
CEDRIC WATTS

WORDSWORTH CLASSICS

In loving memory of
Michael Trayler
the founder of Wordsworth Editions

7

Readers who are interested in other titles from
Wordsworth Editions are invited to visit our website at
www.wordsworth-editions.com

For our latest list and a full mail-order service, contact
Bibliophile Books, 5 Thomas Road, London E14 7BN
TEL: +44 (0)20 7515 9222 FAX: +44 (0)20 7538 4115
E-MAIL: orders@bibliophilebooks.com

First published in 1992 by Wordsworth Editions Limited

8B East Street, Ware, Hertfordshire SG12 9HJ

ISBN 978 1 85326 254 8

Typeset in Great Britain by Antony Gray
Printed and bound by Clays Ltd, St Ives plc

CONTENTS

GENERAL INTRODUCTION

In the Wordsworth Classics' Shakespeare Series, the inaugural volumes are *Romeo and Juliet*, *The Merchant of Venice* and *Henry V*, followed by *A Midsummer Night's Dream*, *Much Ado about Nothing*, *Twelfth Night*, *Hamlet* and *Othello*. Each play in this Shakespeare Series is accompanied by a standard apparatus, including an introduction, explanatory notes and a glossary. The textual editing takes account of recent scholarship while giving the material a careful reappraisal. The apparatus is, however, concise rather than elaborate. We hope that the resultant volumes prove to be handy, reliable and helpful. Above all, we hope that, from Shakespeare's works, readers will derive pleasure, wisdom, provocation, challenges, and insights: insights into his culture and ours, and into the era of civilisation to which his writings have made – and continue to make – such potently influential contributions. Shakespeare's eloquence will, undoubtedly, re-echo 'in states unborn and accents yet unknown'.

CEDRIC WATTS
Series Editor

INTRODUCTION

Shakespeare's *Much Ado about Nothing* [1] is a lively work which is likely to provoke divided responses. Accordingly, this Introduction has two parts. In Part 1, I offer the case against *Much Ado about Nothing* which might be presented by a hostile reader of the play. Part 2 offers the case of someone who enjoys the play.

I

This Fable, absurd and ridiculous as it is, was drawn from the . . . story of *Genevra* in *Ariosto's Orlando Furioso*, a Fiction which, as it is managed by the Epic Poet, is neither improbable nor unnatural; but by *Shakespeare* mangled and defaced, full of Inconsistencies, Contradictions and Blunders.

That's what Charlotte Lennox said of *Much Ado about Nothing* in the eighteenth century.[2] Other critics have echoed her sense of its 'Inconsistencies'. 'The whole of the serious matter of the last act necessarily fails to convince', declared E. K. Chambers. George Brandes remarked: 'If ever man was unworthy a woman's love, that man is Claudio. If ever marriage was odious and ill-omened, this is it.' As for the humour: George Bernard Shaw observed that much of it was 'indecent', stained by 'vulgar naughtiness'.[3] If we thus gather the complaints that critics have, over the years, made about *Much Ado about Nothing*, we may gain the impression that this is one of the worst comedies ever written. And while the critics have complained about the plot, the characterisation and the humour, scholars have revealed textual confusion and puzzling obscurities.

You can soon see what is odd about the plot. It repeatedly thrusts implausibilities at us. Consider the following. In Act 1,

does Claudio personally woo Hero, whom he loves? No: pre-
posterously, he lets a friend, Don Pedro, do the wooing on his
behalf; and this is partly to create a subsequent plot-twist, when
Claudio wrongly thinks that Don Pedro may be treacherously
courting Hero for himself. To us, the most bizarre feature is
surely the readiness of Hero to accept as husband a man whose
feelings are so tepid or pusillanimous that he is unable to woo
her directly but has to use a go-between; and even this interpre-
tation generously assumes that, during the masked ball, she was
able to distinguish between Don Pedro and Claudio – which is
by no means certain. If she was not able to do so, but thought
that Don Pedro was Claudio, she has been wooed on false
pretences, won by love-speeches that were not actually made by
the man who hopes to marry her. In any case, she had gone to
the ball expecting that Don Pedro would court her for himself;
so, if she thought that she was genuinely being wooed by Don
Pedro, it seems implausible that she should then acquiesce in
being handed over, as fiancée, to a quite different man.

Later, Claudio is deceived into thinking that Hero is recklessly
unchaste. Instead of reflecting sceptically on the evidence, or of
asking her promptly for an explanation, he goes along to the
marriage ceremony and there denounces her with brutal vehe-
mence. She is then thought to have died from the shock of the
denunciation. When we next see Claudio, it is in a scene in
which, far from expressing remorse at this tragedy, he joins
Don Pedro in jesting that Benedick will soon be married to an
adulterous wife. Some time afterwards, when Hero's innocence is
established, Claudio swiftly agrees to undertake a penance – which
is that of marrying speedily a woman whom he does not know
(Leonato's 'niece') and has never seen. Thus, having been ruthless
to Hero, he is now unflinchingly willing to undertake a bizarrely
loveless marriage. Of course, the 'niece' turns out to be Hero after
all, and she is quite content to become the bride of the man who
had once wrongly denounced her and who had then blithely
agreed to accept another woman as his wife. Notoriously, one of
the oddest moments in the whole sequence of events comes when
Beatrice, after the scandal has overtaken Hero, exclaims to
Benedick: 'Kill Claudio!' You can understand her anger at
Claudio; neverthless, for the heroine of a Shakespearian comedy

to command her lover to commit murder seems jarringly extreme.

The plots of Elizabethan comedies usually do contain some preposterous stuff, but *Much Ado about Nothing* might well win any prize awarded for the supremely preposterous. Don John is wicked because . . . he is wicked. Here is malignity without any motive-hunting:[4] he does bad things because he likes doing them. Late in the play, it is mentioned that he is illegitimate (and the original stage-directions call him 'John the Bastard'); but, whereas Edmund in *King Lear* seeks in his illegitimacy a rationalisation of his wicked course, no such rationalisation is offered by Don John. Certainly, John claims that Claudio 'hath all the glory of my overthrow': Claudio has gained renown by defeating him; but John declares:

> I had rather be a canker in a hedge than a rose in his grace; and it better fits my blood to be disdained of all, than to fashion a carriage to rob love from any. In this (though I cannot be said to be a flattering honest man), it must not be denied but I am a plain-dealing villain.

Badness is in his blood; and he therefore remains an uninteresting and unconvincing malefactor. Eventually, he is unmasked because, when his wicked plot is discussed by Conrade and Borachio, the dim-witted watchmen just happen to be listening, and arrest these two rogues – who then become remarkably co-operative in the matter of their own arrest. Really, Dogberry, Verges and their associates are so stupid that Conrade and Borachio could easily have talked their way out of the situation; and, in any case, the watchmen have already been instructed that a drunkard (such as Borachio) should be dismissed or ignored.

The most strained contrivance is the crucial scene of apparent infidelity, when Claudio thinks he sees Borachio in an amorous exchange with Hero at her bedroom window. In reality, Borachio is staging a scene with Margaret, who has reluctantly been persuaded to play the part of Hero. How she was persuaded remains obscure: her character is contradictory. In any case, as Lewis Carroll long ago pointed out, how was it possible for Margaret to appear at Hero's bedroom window at all? Hero herself must, for that one night, have been compelled to sleep elsewhere. Her bedfellow for twelve months has been Beatrice, who must have participated in the strange alteration of arrangements. As Carroll says, Beatrice could surely have defended the slandered Hero by saying something like this:

> But, good my lord, sweet Hero slept not there:
> She had another chamber for the nonce.
> 'Twas sure some counterfeit that did present
> Her person at the window, aped her voice,
> Her mien, her manners, and hath thus deceived
> My good lord Pedro and this company . . . [5]

A recent editor comments that this is 'a neat example of the absurdity produced by asking "real" questions of fictitious situations'.[6] The snag is that Shakespeare is often praised for this 'truth to life', for exhibiting what is centrally realistic. Even when dealing with his comedies, critics repeatedly seek to demonstrate that the bed-rock of the works is provided by perennial, observable human features. The crtierion of realism is never wholly absent from Shakespearian criticism. Of course, in comedies we tolerate all sorts of liberties in plotting. What is notable is that *Much Ado about Nothing* seems markedly more strained in its plotting than other comedies which, by their conspicuous stylisation or by the frank incorporation of the supernatural, make suspension of disbelief so much easier. Lacking the elegant artifice of *Love's Labour's Lost* and the magical surrealism of *A Midsummer Night's Dream* or *The Tempest*, *Much Ado* becomes structurally more likely to evoke critical incredulity.

Such incredulity is, for audiences in the twenty-first century, likely to be linked to dismay at the pervasively patriarchal ethos of the work. Poor Hero: denounced by her fiancé and then manipulated by a friar, her father and her uncle; obliged to be given in marriage first as herself, then as someone else, then as herself again; and to be married to a Claudio who, frankly, seems unworthy of her. Certainly, the play appears at least to have a promisingly feminist element in the character of Beatrice. She spars wittily with Benedick, giving as good as she gets, and seems obdurate in defending herself from the claims of matrimony – for a while. Nevertheless, after being perusaded that Benedick loves her but is reluctant to display that love, she concedes that she herself loves him, and conventional marriage prevails after all. So, too, does the patriarchal order. Beatrice's show of independence is a challenge to be met and overcome by traditional conservative forces.

Much Ado is famed for its witty dialogue, particularly that of Beatrice and Benedick. Unfortunately, much of the wit has become obscured, in course of time, by linguistic changes. Even the scholarly editors seem to be perplexed by various passages.[7] Some of the gags are tedious: notably, Dogberry's assumption that 'tedious' is a compliment. More extensive and more tiresome is the horning-stuff. The Elizabethans seem to have been indefatigably delighted by references to the cuckold's horns, those often-invisible horns which supposedly sprouted from the foreheads of cuckolded husbands, men deceived by their adulterous wives. Allusions to such horns abound in *Much Ado*; and these days they are no more topical and funny than are gags from the late 1940s about snoek. Editors can explain them, but a joke explained is a joke extinguished; and recent audiences, while relishing the rude, recoil from the erudite. What is clear is that masculine fear and distrust of the female not only inflect the plot but also pervade the humour of *Much Ado about Nothing*.

Another flaw of the play is the paucity of memorably eloquent speeches. Other Shakespearian comedies of this period (1595–1601) contain a range of speeches which are richly descriptive, emotionally engaging or philosophically memorable (or all three together). *As You Like It*, *A Midsummer Night's Dream*, *Twelfth Night* and *The Merchant of Venice* are thus replete. *Much Ado about Nothing*, in comparison, lacks this abundance. Occasionally the verse glows with descriptive vigour, as when Hero in Act 3, scene 1, muses on the honeysuckle in the pleachèd bower; and, in Act 4, scene 1, Leonato certainly develops an indignant eloquence when lamenting the apparent loss of his daughter's virtue; but generally there is not a textural range and power to rival those other comedies cited. In any case, scholarly evidence shows that the surviving early texts of *Much Ado about Nothing* represent a preliminary stage in the play's evolution: we lack a 'finished', enriched and polished version.[8]

In short, *Much Ado about Nothing* may at first seem unfunny, obscure, implausible, poetically limited, rather heartless, and, on various counts, offensive to women. The next section, however, provides some alternative views.

2

The Victorian poet and critic, Algernon Swinburne, declared in 1879:

> If it is proverbially impossible to determine by selection the greatest work of Shakespeare, it is easy enough to decide on the date and name of his most perfect comic masterpiece. For absolute power of composition, for faultless balance and blameless rectitude of design, there is unquestionably no creation of his hand that will bear comparison with *Much Ado About Nothing*. The ultimate marriage of Hero and Claudio, . . . in itself a doubtfully desirable consummation, makes no flaw in the dramatic perfection of a piece which could not otherwise have been wound up at all.[9]

Anyone who sees a good production of this play soon discovers why it has long been among the more successful of Shakespeare's comedies, popular ever since the seventeenth century. The text of the play provides a basis for diverse interpretations and adaptations by editors, directors and performers. There is no one *Much Ado about Nothing*; there is an ever-increasing number of different works bearing this title. Apparent liabilities in the script (e.g. dated gags or inconsistencies in the plot) can constitute fruitful challenges, to be dealt with by new stage business, by cuts and rearrangements, by modes of stylisation. Indeed, the durability of Shakespearian drama in general is ensured not only by the strengths of the plays but also by their seeming weaknesses, for the latter elicit the imaginative creativity of generation after generation of interpreters. Ingenious editors, directors and actors find ways of aiding the author.

One great strength of *Much Ado about Nothing*, and one of the sources of its popularity, is certainly the potentiality for subtle liveliness in the enactment of the relationship between Beatrice and Benedick. Indeed, from its early days the play has been regarded as *Beatrice and Benedick* rather than as *Much Ado about Nothing*. In 1613 it was termed 'Benedicte and Betteris' in the Lord Treasurer's accounts; in 1632, Charles I wrote 'Benedik and

Betrice' by the title in his copy of the Second Folio edition; and, in 1640, a poetic tribute to Shakespeare by Leonard Digges includes these words:

> let but *Beatrice*
> And *Benedicke* be seene, loe in a trice
> The Cockpit Galleries, Boxes, all are full . . . [10]

Famed pairings of performers of Beatrice and Benedick include Ellen Tree and Charles Kean, Ellen Terry and Henry Irving, Diana Wynyard and Anthony Quayle, Peggy Ashcroft and John Gielgud, Judi Dench and Donald Sinden, Sinead Cusack and Derek Jacobi. John F. Cox's edition of the play shows how diversely the two characters could be interpreted. In Benedick, emphasis might fall either on his witty pugnacity or on an emergent earnest commitment. In Beatrice, the caustic might be dominant, or, instead, a flirtatious challenge. As the twentieth century progressed, characterisations of Beatrice often displayed a new combativeness, reflecting a burgeoning feminism:

> The frequency of powerful, assertive Beatrices in late twentieth-century productions is a manifestation of the broader cultural tendency for women to perceive themselves as no longer subordinate or submissive.[11]

Numerous productions have also shown, of course, that both Benedick and Beatrice, while capable of energetic wit-combats, evince a vulnerability and a need for love. Each has a layered personality; and the actors can establish new balances or imbalances in the combination of characteristics. Indeed, Benedick and Beatrice, in their multiple theatrical manifestations, constitute a family: recurrent features provide its identity, but the family is constantly procreating and evolving

During the twentieth century, again, critics sometimes sensed that *Much Ado about Nothing* might be regarded as a 'problem play', having affinities with at least two other problematic comedies. As John Turner remarked:

> *Much Ado About Nothing*, like *Measure for Measure* and *All's Well That Ends Well*, is best considered as a problem play, whose disturbing ending dramatises the inadequacy of the

ideology by which its ruling classes rule. It is a comedy of social manners whose romance structure, with its improbable plot, characters and denouement, makes deliberate play out of social tensions which in real life are not so readily resolved. For Shakespeare's theatre by its very nature is an arena in which taboos are lifted, moral codes historicised and different social formations scrutinised.[12]

Since the 1960s, various productions, accordingly, have stressed ambiguity. In a production by Franco Zeffirelli, the festive ending was distinctly qualified:

> stop-start interruptions highlighted the discordant elements cutting across the prevailing festivity. After the 'riotous, orgiastic, fancy-dress celebration' of Zeffirelli's finale, the lights and dancers faded away, leaving Don Pedro seated alone, smoking and gazing wistfully into the distance, the festivities finally 'puffed out into nothingness by a single flicker of [his] sceptical cigar' . . . [13]

Don Pedro was left similarly isolated and melancholic at the conclusion of several subsequent productions, notably those by Terry Hands (1982) and John Bell (1996). Other dark features which could readily be emphasised included the malignity of Don John, Hero's harsh treatment at the broken wedding, and the operations of manipulative power. Of course, if that manipulative (and often patriarchal) power is troubling, Shakespeare's script has provided the means to expose it as such.

Trevor Nunn, a distinguished director, once said in an interview: 'The text that I didn't trust, and should have trusted, was *Much Ado About Nothing.*'[14] Shakespeare wrote his plays as scripts for performance, and the main critical test is whether they succeed as performances. In recent times, *Much Ado* has repeatedly been revived on stage, and film productions and videos have also brought it renewed life. A fluently confident adaptation for the screen, directed by Kenneth Branagh, appeared in 1993 and gained general acclaim. Branagh played Benedick to Emma Thompson's Beatrice. Daniel Rosenthal found this an example of exuberant film-making, a lively, radiant, imaginative production. He comments:

It's the 'merry war' between this pair [Benedick and Beatrice] that has ensured *Much Ado*'s lofty reputation amongst the comedies, and Branagh and Thompson, still husband and wife at the time, enjoy their verbal jousts. Branagh could be less self-conscious in his soliloquies, but there's no faulting Thompson, who balances 'clear intelligence and deep vulnerability' (*Daily Mail*) to suggest Beatrice's pleasant, spirited nature and her fear of being left on the shelf.[15]

The film was commercially as well as critically successful. Rosenthal states that it recouped its budget in the UK alone (where the box-office brought in £5,400,000) and took 22 million dollars in the USA (where it was the most successful British film of the year).[16] If you watch a video of that film, you will find that it is still predominantly delightful, vital and vivid, its sombre and sinister elements giving way to the richly celebratory. It sprang effective comic surprises (even if Dogberry seemed deranged), the camera-work was adroit, Thompson was entrancing, and the two plots became intimately linked (showing that 'it takes Claudio's immature and cruel disruption of the socially sanctioned ritual of marriage to spur the creation of Beatrice and Benedick's privately conceived and imagined ceremony of reconciliation'[17]). Malign deception and substitution were encompassed and defeated by benign deception and substitution. Though the adaptation was bold and took liberties with the text, Shakespeare would probably not have minded: after all, he too repeatedly took liberties with the source-material of his plays. If the Shakespearian drama remains problematic, the Branagh production was proof that the work's tensions and divisions could nevertheless gain joyous local resolution.

Russ McDonald once remarked:

> Shakespeare is the master of the combined response. All his comedies are hybrids, complicated mixtures of farce and romance, sunshine and shadow, absurdity and profundity.[18]

The protean nature of *Much Ado about Nothing* is amply illustrated in John Cox's edition, which, drawing on a wealth of reports, reviews and prompt-books, shows how diversely scenes, speeches and even individual phrases have been interpreted in

different productions. We may even infer that every production
of *Much Ado* is a re-writing of it. Indeed, some directors, while
cutting Shakespeare's dialogue, have added new dialogue of their
own. The play's dated jests about cuckolds' horns often receive a
pruning, as do such obscure lines as those about the recheat and
the invisible baldric. Scene 2 of Act 1 has sometimes been
deleted entirely. As for additions: in the first scene of a Henry
Irving production in 1891, Don Pedro drew attention to the
spectacular set by remarking 'What a beautiful place you have
here, Signor Leonato.'[19] Again, adaptation can make Claudio
seem relatively cruel or relatively sympathetic. Don John's
motivation can be strengthened by making him a frustrated rival
for Hero's affections. (In a 1904–5 production, 'Claudio, crossing
to exit with Hero [in scene 1], was intercepted by Don John,
who escorted Hero off, leaving a disappointed Claudio gazing
after her.'[20]) Margaret, her part in the conspiracy having been
revealed, can be made to seem more remorseful than the text
suggests: the BBC's televised version in 1984 foregrounded a
weeping Margaret at the opening of Act 5, scene 4. Of course,
there are numerous opportunities for clarifying the plot. For
instance: in a production at Sydney in 1996, Antonio and
Borachio appeared upstairs at separate entrances during the
dialogue between Don Pedro and Claudio at 1.1.280–88. Antonio
heard only enough to believe that Pedro would woo Hero for
himself, whereas Borachio stayed to hear the assurance that the
wooing would be for Claudio. This additional stage-business
explained the discrepancy between the subsequent reports given
by Antonio in Act 1, scene 2, and Borachio in Act 1, scene 3.
Another example of effective adaptation occurred in an Edinburgh
Festival production in 1993. During the scene of lamentation at
the monument, a disguised Hero observed Claudio's mourning:
an innovation which made the eventual reconciliation of Hero
and Claudio the more credible and satisfactory.[21]

In such ways, *Much Ado about Nothing*, for all its courtly elegance,
proves to be a very democratic work: because, down the years, it
invokes the collaboration of so many people who all, gladly joining
forces with Shakespeare, renew and rejuvenate the play. Like the
men of the watch, any of us may help to effect a happy outcome.

NOTES TO THE INTRODUCTION

1 In conformity with the standard bibliographical convention that prepositions in titles are not capitalised (unless they begin those titles), I give 'about' with no initial capital. The Oxford Guide to Style, by R. M. Ritter (Oxford: Oxford University Press, 2002), says that 'very short titles may look best with every word capitalized: All About Eve', but Much Ado about Nothing does not qualify as 'very short'. Nevertheless, numerous previous editors and commentators have capitalised the title of Shakespeare's play as Much Ado About Nothing. Consequently, when quoting or listing the title as given by others, I follow whichever convention is there used.

2 Charlotte Lennox: Shakespear Illustrated (1763–4), quoted in Shakespeare: The Critical Heritage, ed. Brian Vickers, Vol. 4 (London: Routledge, 1976), p. 140.

3 E. K. Chambers: Shakespeare: A Survey (London: Sidgwick & Jackson, 1926, rpt. 1963), pp. 134–5. George Brandes: William Shakespeare: A Critical Study (London: Heinemann, 1902), p. 217. George Bernard Shaw: Shaw on Shakespeare, ed. Edwin Wilson (London: Cassell, 1962), pp. 135-7.

4 Samuel Coleridge said that Iago, in Shakespeare's Othello, manifested 'the motive-hunting of motiveless malignity'. See Coleridge: Shakespearean Criticism, ed. T. M. Raysor, Vol. 1 (London: Dent, 1906), p. 44.

5 The Letters of Lewis Carroll, ed. Morton N. Cohen, Vol. 1 (London: Macmillan, 1979), pp. 489–90; quotation, p. 489. In what is probably Shakespeare's main source for the play, Matteo Bandello's Italian tale of Timbreo and Fenicia, there is no impersonation of the lady by a female servant.

6 Much Ado About Nothing, ed. F. H. Mares (Cambridge: Cambridge University Press, 1988), p. 157.

7 For example, at 2.1.33–4, Beatrice talks of leading apes into hell (a proverbial fate for an unmarried woman), and a baffled editor remarks: 'No explanation has been found for this odd commonplace'. (See Much Ado About Nothing, ed. Sheldon P. Zitner; Oxford: Oxford University Press, 1993; p. 114.)

8 See the part of this volume entitled 'Acknowledgements and Textual Matters'.

9 A. C. Swinburne: A Study of Shakespeare [1879] (London: Heinemann, 1918), p. 153.

10 Quoted in *Much Ado About Nothing*, ed. John F. Cox (Cambridge: Cambridge University Press, 1997), p. 4.

11 Cox, pp. 66–7. Benedick and Beatrice are literary descendants of Berowne and Rosaline in *Love's Labour's Lost*, a markedly feministic play.

12 John Turner: 'Claudio and the Code of Honour' in *Critical Essays on 'Much Ado About Nothing'*, ed. Linda Cookson and Bryan Loughrey (Harlow: Longman, 1989), p. 29.

13 Cox, p. 235.

14 Nunn is quoted in Ralph Berry: *On Directing Shakespeare* (London: Hamish Hamilton, 1989), p. 78.

15 Daniel Rosenthal: *Shakespeare on Screen* (London: Hamlyn, 2000), p. 162.

16 Rosenthal, p. 162.

17 Samuel Crowl: 'Flamboyant Realist: Kenneth Branagh' in *The Cambridge Companion to Shakespeare on Film*, ed. Russell Jackson (Cambridge: Cambridge University Press, 2000), p. 231.

18 Russ McDonald: *The Bedford Companion to Shakespeare* (Basingstoke: Macmillan, 1996), p. 155.

19 Cox, p. 91. Other directors (notably David Garrick and Franco Zeffirelli) substituted their own dialogue where they thought Shakespeare's was obscure.

20 Cox, p. 97.

21 Cox, pp. 102–3, 224.

FURTHER READING
(in chronological order)

George Bernard Shaw: reviews (1898 and 1905) of *Much Ado about Nothing*, reprinted in *Shaw on Shakespeare*, ed. Edwin Wilson. London: Cassell, 1962.

Narrative and Dramatic Sources of Shakespeare, Vol. II, ed. Geoffrey Bullough. London: Routledge & Kegan Paul; New York: Columbia University Press, 1958.

G. K. Hunter: *Shakespeare: The Later Comedies*. London: Longmans, Green, 1962.

F. E. Halliday: *A Shakespeare Companion 1564–1964*. Harmondsworth: Penguin, 1964.

J. R. Mulryne: *Shakespeare: Much Ado About Nothing*. London: Arnold, 1965.

Shakespeare's Comedies: An Anthology of Modern Criticism, ed. Laurence Lerner. Harmondsworth: Penguin, 1967.

Ralph Berry: *Shakespeare's Comedies: Explorations in Form*. Princeton, N.J.: Princeton University Press, 1972.

Samuel Schoenbaum: *William Shakespeare: A Compact Documentary Life* [1977]. Revised edition: New York and Oxford: Oxford University Press, 1987.

Ralph Berry: *On Directing Shakespeare: Interviews with Contemporary Directors*. London: Hamish Hamilton, 1989.

Shakespeare: 'Much Ado About Nothing' and 'As You Like It': A Casebook, ed. John Russell Brown. Basingstoke: Macmillan, 1979; rpt., Basingstoke: Palgrave, 2002.

The Woman's Part: Feminist Criticism of Shakespeare, ed. C. R. S. Lenz, G. Greene and C. T. Neely. Urbana, Ill., and London: University of Illinois Press, 1980.

Arthur Kirsch: *Shakespeare and the Experience of Love*. Cambridge: Cambridge University Press, 1981.

Richard A. Levin: *Love and Society in Shakespearean Comedy*. London and Toronto: Associated University Presses, 1985.

Carol Thomas Neely: *Broken Nuptials in Shakespeare's Plays*. New Haven and London: Yale University Press, 1985.

The Cambridge Companion to Shakespeare Studies, ed. Stanley Wells. Cambridge: Cambridge University Press, 1986.

Roger Sales: *William Shakespeare: 'Much Ado About Nothing'*. Harmondsworth: Penguin, 1987.

Kristian Smidt: *Unconfomities in Shakespeare's Later Comedies*. Basingstoke: Macmillan, 1993.

Russ McDonald: *The Bedford Companion to Shakespeare: An Introduction with Documents*. Basingstoke: Macmillan, 1996.

The Cambridge Companion to Shakespeare on Film, ed. Russell Jackson. Cambridge: Cambridge University Press, 2000.

Daniel Rosenthal: *Shakespeare on Screen*. London: Hamlyn, 2000.

The Cambridge Companion to Shakespeare, ed. Margreta de Grazia and Stanley Wells. Cambridge: Cambridge University Press, 2001.

NOTE ON SHAKESPEARE

William Shakespeare was the son of a glover at Stratford-upon-Avon, and tradition gives his date of birth as 23 April, 1564; certainly, three days later, he was christened at the parish church. It is likely that he attended the local Grammar School but had no university education. Of his early career there is no record, though John Aubrey reports a claim that he was a rural schoolmaster. In 1582 Shakespeare married Anne Hathaway, with whom he had two daughters, Susanna and Judith, and a son, Hamnet, who died in 1596. How he became involved with the stage in London is uncertain, but by 1592 he was sufficiently established as a playwright to be criticised in print as a challengingly versatile 'upstart Crow'. He was a leading member of the Lord Chamberlain's company, which became the King's Men on the accession of James I in 1603. Being not only a playwright and actor but also a 'sharer' (one of the owners of the company, entitled to a share of the profits), Shakespeare prospered greatly, as is proven by the numerous records of his financial transactions. Towards the end of his life, he loosened his ties with London and retired to New Place, the large house in Stratford which he had bought in 1597. He died on 23 April, 1616, and is buried in the place of his baptism, Holy Trinity Church. The earliest collected edition of his plays, the First Folio, was published in 1623, and its prefatory verse-tributes include Ben Jonson's famous declaration, 'He was not of an age, but for all time'.

ACKNOWLEDGEMENTS AND TEXTUAL MATTERS

I have consulted – and am indebted to – numerous editions of *Much Ado about* (or *About*) *Nothing*, notably those by Horace Howard Furness (Philadelphia: Lippincott, 1899; reprinted, New York: Dover, 1964); Sir Arthur Quiller-Couch and John Dover Wilson ('The New Shakespeare': London: Cambridge University Press, 1923; revised and reprinted, 1953; revised and abridged as 'The Cambridge Pocket Shakespeare', 1959); R. A. Foakes (Harmondsworth: Penguin, 1968); G. Blakemore Evans *et al.* (*The Riverside Shakespeare*: Boston, Mass.: Houghton Mifflin, 1974); A. R. Humphreys (the Arden Shakespeare: London and New York: Methuen, 1981); Stanley Wells and Gary Taylor (*The Complete Works*: Oxford: Oxford University Press, 1986); F. H. Mares (the New Cambridge Shakespeare: Cambridge: Cambridge University Press, 1988); Sheldon P. Zitner (the Oxford Shakespeare: Oxford: Oxford University Press, 1993); John F. Cox (Cambridge: Cambridge University Press, 1997); and Stephen Greenblatt *et al.* (*The Norton Shakespeare*: New York and London: Norton, 1997). Professor Mario Curreli provided wise advice.

A 'quarto' is a book with relatively small pages, each about 9 by 7 inches (23 by 18 cm.), while a 'folio' is a book with relatively large pages, each about 14 by 9 inches (36 by 23 cm.). A quarto volume is made of sheets of paper, each of which has been folded twice to form four leaves (and thus eight pages), whereas each of a folio's sheets has been folded once to form two leaves (and thus four pages). *Much Ado about Nothing* was possibly first performed in the winter of 1598-9, and the earliest printed text of the play is the 1600 Quarto (Q): *Much adoe about Nothing. As it hath been sundrie times publikely acted by the right honourable, the Lord*

Chamberlaine his seruants. Written by William Shakespeare. This Q text seems to derive from 'foul papers', i.e., an untidy manuscript by the playwright, or a copy of it. Some features suggest that Shakespeare worked by trial and error: there are various loose ends and inconsistencies in the play. These include named but silent characters, inconsistent speech-prefixes, and absent entrances and exits. Some small changes were made during the print-run of that Quarto text. Then, in 1623, appeared the First Folio (F): the first 'Collected Edition' of Shakespeare's works. The version of *Much Ado* which appears in this Folio volume does not seem to have independent Shakespearian authority, though there are numerous small variants. Some of them (e.g. the substitution of '*Iacke Wilson*' for Q's '*Musicke*' in one stage direction) show the influence of the playhouse. It is probable that the F text (which introduces both minor corrections and minor mistakes) was based on a copy of Q which had been lightly emended as the result of a cursory comparison with a manuscript prompt-book. A remarkably large number of Q's errors and oddities has been preserved by F: examples include the name 'Peter' (for 'Pedro') in Act 1, scene 1, the speech-prefix '*Couley*' (for '*Conrade*') at 4.2.67, and a premature '*Exeunt*' direction for Leonato and Antonio at 5.1.107 instead of 108.

When commenting on the Quarto version, F. H. Mares (in his 1988 Cambridge edition, p. 148) rightly says:

> There are inconsistencies within the text both on a large scale (characters who are introduced to no purpose, statements made at one point which are contradicted at another) and in smaller detail (variant spellings, inconsistency in the naming of characters, missing or inadequate stage directions). What the text offers, in short, is a becoming, a process, not a finished product.

Examples of inconsistency include the following. First: Hero's mother, Innogen, is given two entries into the action but never speaks. (Other editors exclude her; I retain her.) Secondly: in Q's version of Act 2, scene 1, Leonato's brother has the speech-prefix '*brother*', and Ursula dances with a 'signior Anthonio' who has the speech-prefix '*Antho.*'. Two male characters or one? In Act 5, scene 1, the brother is named 'Brother Anthony'. An eighteenth-century editor, Nicholas Rowe, accordingly assumed that only one character was indicated by these various references, and other editors have followed Rowe's unifying example. Thirdly: in Act 1, scene 2, Leonato's brother has a son, but, in Act 5, scene 1, Hero is the sole heir of both Antonio and Leonato: the son has been eliminated. A graver problem, as we have noted in the Introduction, was raised by Lewis Carroll. Furthermore, scene 3 of Act 5 provides an interesting example of the ways in which editors 'improve' the play when the early scripts do not do what the editors expect.

If we look at that 'mourning' scene in the 1981 Arden text, we find that the people who enter are Claudio, Don Pedro, three or four men with tapers, Balthasar and a group of musicians. Claudio reads from a scroll a poem of lamentation for Hero. Balthasar sings the song 'Pardon, goddess of the night', and Claudio rounds it off by saying: 'Now unto thy bones good night! / Yearly will I do this rite.' All this seems very satisfactory: Claudio is mourning as we would expect. Numerous other editors have similarly allocated the speeches. If, however, we consult Q, we find a strangely different scene. The entrants are *Claudio, Prince, and three or foure with tapers*. No Balthasar and no musicians are specified. The person who reads the poem is not Claudio but an anonymous *Lord*. Then Claudio says: 'Now musick sound & sing your solemne hymne' (implying the presence of musicians). The singers, who are not identified by any speech-prefix, are presumably the *three or foure* taper-bearers. After the song, there follow the words 'Now vnto thy bones good night, yeerely will I do this right': these, however, are allocated not to Claudio but to *Lo.*, evidently an abbreviation of *Lord* (so the taper-bearers may retrospectively be termed *lords* by a modern editor). The F text has small variants in spelling and punctuation but otherwise is the same. So here is an obvious editorial problem. You can see that the standard adaptation of the scene by editors makes Claudio more prominent and deepens his character, emphasising his mourning for the supposedly dead Hero. Such adaptation takes great liberties with the early textual matter in order to push the action towards conventionality. This Wordsworth edition chooses to respect the original speech-allocations of this scene. Of course, they may be faulty, as they sometimes are elsewhere; but I believe that such fidelity preserves the elegiac qualities of the scene and heightens its strangeness. Furthermore, by not markedly softening Claudio, it makes him here relatively consistent with the rather callous Claudio seen previously. He had wooed by proxy; let him mourn by proxy, too. Thus, the various anomalies and oddities of Q and F provide challenges and opportunities not only for editors but also for critics and directors of the play.

The present edition of *Much Ado about Nothing* represents a practical compromise between the early texts, Shakespeare's intentions (insofar as they can be reasonably inferred) and modern requirements. In the interests of fidelity to Shakespeare's likely usages, I have retained certain archaisms which some other editions modernise. For instance, this text keeps the spellings 'Signior' and 'Millaine'. Some editions change 'Signior' to 'Signor', but that is not always the correct Italian (*Signore*). Shakespeare pronounced 'Millaine' with stress on the first syllable, unlike the modern 'Milan'. I have also preserved the occasional use of 'and' to mean 'if ' and of 'a' to mean 'he'. The glossary explains such archaisms and unfamiliar terms, while the annotations offer clarification of obscurities. No edition of the play can claim to be definitive, but this one – aiming at clarity and concise practicality – can promise to be very useful.

MUCH ADO ABOUT NOTHING

CHARACTERS IN THE PLAY

LEONATO, *Governor of Messina.*

INNOGEN, *his wife.*

ANTONIO, *Leonato's brother.*

HERO, *Leonato's daughter.*

BEATRICE, *Leonato's niece.*

MARGARET *and* URSULA, *gentlewomen attending Hero.*

DON PEDRO *(initially* DON PETER*), Prince of Arragon.*

CLAUDIO, *a gentleman, companion of Don Pedro.*

BENEDICK, *another gentleman, companion of Don Pedro.*

BOY *serving Benedick.*

BALTHASAR, *a singer attending Don Pedro.*

DON JOHN, *illegitimate brother of Don Pedro.*

BORACHIO *and* CONRADE, *followers of Don John.*

FRIAR FRANCIS.

DOGBERRY, *constable in charge of the Watch.*

VERGES, *the Headborough, Dogberry's partner.*

SEVERAL WATCHMEN.

SEXTON.

KINSMAN *of Leonato.*

LORDS, COURTIERS, SOLDIERS *and* ATTENDANTS.

MUSICIANS *and* SINGERS.

The general location: Messina in Sicily.

MUCH ADO ABOUT NOTHING[1]

ACT I, SCENE I.

Leonato's garden.[2]

Enter LEONATO, *Governor of Messina,* INNOGEN (*his wife*), HERO (*his daughter*), *and* BEATRICE (*his niece*), *with a* MESSENGER.[3]

LEONATO   I learn in this letter that Don Peter of Arragon[4] comes this night to Messina.

MESSEN.   He is very near by this; he was not three leagues off when I left him.

LEONATO   How many gentlemen have you lost in this action?

MESSEN.   But few of any sort, and none of name.

LEONATO   A victory is twice itself when the achiever brings home full numbers. I find here that Don Peter hath bestowed much honour on a young Florentine called Claudio.   10

MESSEN.   Much deserved on his part, and equally remembered by Don Pedro. He hath borne himself beyond the promise of his age, doing in the figure of a lamb the feats of a lion. He hath indeed better bettered expectation than you must expect of me to tell you how.

LEONATO   He hath an uncle here in Messina will be very much glad of it.

MESSEN.   I have already delivered him letters, and there appears much joy in him, even so much that joy could not show itself modest enough without a badge of bitterness.   20

LEONATO   Did he break out into tears?

MESSEN.   In great measure.

LEONATO   A kind overflow of kindness: there are no faces truer than those that are so washed. How much better is it to weep at joy than to joy at weeping!

BEATRICE   I pray you, is Signior Mountanto[5] returned from the wars or no?

MESSEN.   I know none of that name, lady. There was none such in the army of any sort.

LEONATO	What is he that you ask for, niece?

30

HERO	My cousin means Signior Benedick of Padua.
MESSEN.	O, he's returned, and as pleasant as ever he was.
BEATRICE	He set up his bills here in Messina and challenged Cupid at the flight, and my uncle's Fool, reading the challenge, subscribed for Cupid and challenged him at the birdbolt.[6] I pray you, how many hath he killed and eaten in these wars? But how many hath he killed? For indeed I promised to eat all of his killing.
LEONATO	Faith, niece, you tax Signior Benedick too much, but he'll be meet with you, I doubt it not.

40

MESSEN.	He hath done good service, lady, in these wars.
BEATRICE	You had musty victual, and he hath holp to eat it: he is a very valiant trencher-man; he hath an excellent stomach.[7]
MESSEN.	And a good soldier too, lady.
BEATRICE	And a good soldier to a lady, but what is he to a lord?
MESSEN.	A lord to a lord, a man to a man; stuffed with all honourable virtues.
BEATRICE	It is so, indeed: he is no less than a stuffed man; but, for the stuffing – well, we are all mortal.

50

LEONATO	You must not, sir, mistake my niece. There is a kind of merry war betwixt Signior Benedick and her: they never meet but there's a skirmish of wit between them.
BEATRICE	Alas, he gets nothing by that. In our last conflict, four of his five wits went halting off, and now is the whole man governed with one: so that if he have wit enough to keep himself warm, let him bear it for a difference between himself and his horse; for it is all the wealth that he hath left, to be known a reasonable creature. Who is his companion now? He hath every month a new sworn brother.

60

MESSEN.	Is't possible?
BEATRICE	Very easily possible: he wears his faith but as the fashion of his hat: it ever changes with the next block.
MESSEN.	I see, lady, the gentleman is not in your books.
BEATRICE	No; and he were,[8] I would burn my study. But I pray you, who is his companion? Is there no young squarer now that will make a voyage with him to the devil?

MESSEN.   He is most in the company of the right noble Claudio.

BEATRICE   O Lord, he will hang upon him like a disease: he is 70
           sooner caught than the pestilence, and the taker runs
           presently mad. God help the noble Claudio, if he have
           caught the Benedick: it will cost him a thousand
           pound ere a be cured.[9]

MESSEN.   I will hold friends with you, lady.

BEATRICE   Do, good friend.

LEONATO   *You* will never run mad, niece.

BEATRICE   No, not till a hot January.

MESSEN.   Don Pedro is approached.

Enter DON PEDRO, CLAUDIO, BENEDICK, BALTHASAR
    and DON JOHN (*'the bastard'*).[10]

D. PEDRO   Good Signior Leonato, are you come to meet your 80
           trouble? The fashion of the world is to avoid cost, and
           you encounter it.

LEONATO   Never came trouble to my house in the likeness of
           your Grace; for trouble being gone, comfort should
           remain; but when you depart from me, sorrow abides,
           and happiness takes his leave.

D. PEDRO   You embrace your charge too willingly. I think this is
           your daughter.

LEONATO   Her mother hath many times told me so.

BENEDICK   Were you in doubt, sir, that you asked her?   90

LEONATO   Signior Benedick, no, for then were you a child.

D. PEDRO   You have it full, Benedick; we may guess by this what
           you are, being a man. Truly the lady fathers herself.[11]
           Be happy, lady, for you are like an honourable father.
                        [*He talks privately with Hero and Leonato.*

BENEDICK   If Signior Leonato be her father, she would not have
           his head on her shoulders for all Messina, as like him as
           she is.

BEATRICE   I wonder that you will still be talking, Signior Bene-
           dick: nobody marks you.

BENEDICK   What, my dear Lady Disdain! Are you yet living?   100

BEATRICE   Is it possible Disdain should die, while she hath such
           meet food to feed it as Signior Benedick? Courtesy
           itself must convert to Disdain, if you come in her
           presence.

BENEDICK Then is Courtesy a turncoat; but it is certain I am
loved of all ladies, only you excepted; and I would I
could find in my heart that I had not a hard heart, for
truly I love none.

BEATRICE A dear happiness to women – they would else have
been troubled with a pernicious suitor. I thank God 110
and my cold blood, I am of your humour for that; I
had rather hear my dog bark at a crow than a man
swear he loves me.

BENEDICK God keep your ladyship still in that mind, so some
gentleman or other shall scape a predestinate scratched
face.

BEATRICE Scratching could not make it worse, and 'twere such a
face as yours were.

BENEDICK Well, you are a rare parrot-teacher.

BEATRICE A bird of my tongue is better than a beast of yours.[12]   120

BENEDICK I would my horse had the speed of your tongue, and so
good a continuer; but keep your way, a God's name: I
have done.

BEATRICE You always end with a jade's trick. I know you of old.

D. PEDRO That is the sum of all, Leonato. [*He turns.*] Signior
Claudio and Signior Benedick, my dear friend Leonato
hath invited you all. I tell him we shall stay here at the
least a month, and he heartily prays some occasion may
detain us longer. I dare swear he is no hypocrite, but
prays from his heart.   130

LEONATO If you swear, my lord, you shall not be forsworn. [*To
Don John:*] Let me bid you welcome, my lord: being
reconciled to the Prince your brother,[13] I owe you all
duty.

DON JOHN I thank you. I am not of many words, but I thank you.

LEONATO Please it your Grace lead on?

D. PEDRO Your hand, Leonato: we will go together.

                    [*Exeunt all except Benedick and Claudio.*

CLAUDIO Benedick, didst thou note the daughter of Signior
Leonato?

BENEDICK I noted her not, but I looked on her.   140

CLAUDIO Is she not a modest young lady?

BENEDICK Do you question me as an honest man should do, for

           my simple true judgement? Or would you have me
           speak after my custom, as being a professed tyrant to
           their sex?

CLAUDIO   No, I pray thee speak in sober judgement.

BENEDICK   Why, i'faith, methinks she's too low for a high praise,
           too brown for a fair praise, and too little for a great
           praise. Only this commendation I can afford her, that
           were she other than she is, she were unhandsome, and   150
           being no other but as she is, I do not like her.

CLAUDIO   Thou thinkest I am in sport. I pray thee tell me truly
           how thou lik'st her.

BENEDICK   Would you buy her, that you inquire after her?

CLAUDIO   Can the world buy such a jewel?

BENEDICK   Yea, and a case to put it into. But speak you this with a
           sad brow? Or do you play the flouting Jack, to tell us
           Cupid is a good hare-finder, and Vulcan a rare carpenter?
           Come, in what key shall a man take you to go in the
           song?[14]   160

CLAUDIO   In mine eye, she is the sweetest lady that ever I looked
           on.

BENEDICK   I can see yet without spectacles, and I see no such
           matter: there's her cousin, and she were not possessed
           with a fury, exceeds her as much in beauty as the first
           of May doth the last of December. But I hope you
           have no intent to turn husband, have you?

CLAUDIO   I would scarce trust myself, though I had sworn the
           contrary, if Hero would be my wife.

BENEDICK   Is't come to this? In faith, hath not the world one man   170
           but he will wear his cap with suspicion? Shall I never
           see a bachelor of threescore again? Go to, i'faith, and
           thou wilt needs thrust thy neck into a yoke, wear the
           print of it, and sigh away Sundays.[15]

                            Enter DON PEDRO.[16]

           Look, Don Pedro is returned to seek you.

D. PEDRO   What secret hath held you here, that you followed not
           to Leonato's?

BENEDICK   I would your Grace would constrain me to tell.

D. PEDRO   I charge thee on thy allegiance.

BENEDICK   You hear, Count Claudio. I can be secret as a dumb   180

man; I would have you think so; but, on my allegiance
(mark you this, on my allegiance) – [*to Don Pedro:*] he
is in love! With who? Now that is your Grace's part.
Mark, how short his answer is: with Hero, Leonato's
short daughter.

CLAUDIO   If this were so, so were it uttered.

BENEDICK   Like the old tale, my lord. 'It is not so, nor 'twas not
so; but indeed, God forbid it should be so.'[17]

CLAUDIO   If my passion change not shortly, God forbid it should
be otherwise.   190

D. PEDRO   Amen, if you love her, for the lady is very well worthy.

CLAUDIO   You speak this to fetch me in, my lord.

D. PEDRO   By my troth, I speak my thought.

CLAUDIO   And in faith, my lord, I spoke mine.

BENEDICK   And by my two faiths and troths, my lord, I spoke
mine.

CLAUDIO   That I love her, I feel.

D. PEDRO   That she is worthy, I know.

BENEDICK   That I neither feel how she should be loved, nor know
how she should be worthy, is the opinion that fire   200
cannot melt out of me; I will die in it at the stake.

D. PEDRO   Thou wast ever an obstinate heretic in the despite of
beauty.

CLAUDIO   And never could maintain his part, but in the force of
his will.

BENEDICK   That a woman conceived me, I thank her; that she
brought me up, I likewise give her most humble
thanks; but that I will have a recheat winded in my
forehead, or hang my bugle in an invisible baldric, all
women shall pardon me.[18] Because I will not do them 210
the wrong to mistrust any, I will do myself the right to
trust none: and the fine is (for the which I may go the
finer) I will live a bachelor.

D. PEDRO   I shall see thee, ere I die, look pale with love.

BENEDICK   With anger, with sickness, or with hunger, my lord;
not with love. Prove that ever I lose more blood with
love than I will get again with drinking, pick out mine
eyes with a ballad-maker's pen, and hang me up at the
door of a brothel-house for the sign of blind Cupid.[19]

D. PEDRO   Well, if ever thou dost fall from this faith, thou wilt 220
           prove a notable argument.
BENEDICK   If I do, hang me in a bottle like a cat and shoot at me,
           and he that hits me, let him be clapped on the shoulder
           and called Adam.[20]
D. PEDRO   Well, as time shall try:
           'In time the savage bull doth bear the yoke.'[21]
BENEDICK   The savage bull may, but if ever the sensible Benedick
           bear it, pluck off the bull's horns and set them in my
           forehead, and let me be vildly painted; and in such
           great letters as they write, 'Here is good horse to hire', 230
           let them signify under my sign, 'Here you may see
           Benedick the married man.'
CLAUDIO   If this should ever happen, thou wouldst be horn-mad.
D. PEDRO   Nay, if Cupid have not spent all his quiver in Venice,
           thou wilt quake for this shortly.
BENEDICK   I look for an earthquake too, then.
D. PEDRO   Well, you will temporize with the hours.[22] In the
           meantime, good Signior Benedick, repair to Leonato's,
           commend me to him, and tell him I will not fail him at
           supper; for indeed he hath made great preparation. 240
BENEDICK   I have almost matter enough in me for such an
           embassage, and so I commit you –
CLAUDIO   To the tuition of God; from my house if I had it
D. PEDRO   The sixth of July; your loving friend, Benedick.
BENEDICK   Nay, mock not, mock not. The body of your discourse
           is sometime guarded with fragments, and the guards
           are but slightly basted on neither. Ere you flout old
           ends any further, examine your conscience; and so I
           leave you.[23]   [Exit.
CLAUDIO   My liege, your Highness now may do me good. 250
D. PEDRO   My love is thine to teach. Teach it but how,
           And thou shalt see how apt it is to learn
           Any hard lesson that may do thee good.
CLAUDIO   Hath Leonato any son, my lord?
D. PEDRO   No child but Hero; she's his only heir.
           Dost thou affect her, Claudio?
CLAUDIO   O my lord,
           When you went onward on this ended action,

I looked upon her with a soldier's eye,
That liked, but had a rougher task in hand
Than to drive liking to the name of love;   260
But now I am returned, and that war-thoughts
Have left their places vacant, in their rooms
Come thronging soft and delicate desires,
All prompting me how fair young Hero is,
Saying I liked her ere I went to wars.

D. PEDRO Thou wilt be like a lover presently,
And tire the hearer with a book of words.
If thou dost love fair Hero, cherish it,
And I will break with her, and with her father,
And thou shalt have her.[24] Was't not to this end   270
That thou began'st to twist so fine a story?

CLAUDIO How sweetly you do minister to love,
That know love's grief by his complexion![25]
But lest my liking might too sudden seem,
I would have salved it with a longer treatise.

D. PEDRO What need the bridge much broader than the flood?
The fairest grant is the necessity.[26]
Look, what will serve is fit: 'tis once, thou lovest,
And I will fit thee with the remedy.
I know we shall have revelling tonight: 280
I will assume thy part in some disguise,
And tell fair Hero I am Claudio,
And in her bosom I'll unclasp my heart,
And take her hearing prisoner with the force
And strong encounter of my amorous tale;
Then after to her father will I break,
And the conclusion is, she shall be thine.
In practice let us put it presently.

                                                        [*Exeunt.*

SCENE 2.

In Leonato's house.

Enter, separately, LEONATO *and* ANTONIO (*an old man*), *meeting.*²¹

LEONATO How now, brother, where is my cousin, your son? Hath he provided this music?

ANTONIO He is very busy about it; but brother, I can tell you strange news that you yet dreamt not of.

LEONATO Are they good?

ANTONIO As the event stamps them, but they have a good cover: they show well outward. The Prince and Count Claudio, walking in a thick-pleached alley in mine orchard, were thus much overheard by a man of mine: the Prince discovered to Claudio that he loved my 10 niece, your daughter, and meant to acknowledge it this night in a dance; and if he found her accordant, he meant to take the present time by the top, and instantly break with you of it.²⁸

LEONATO Hath the fellow any wit that told you this?

ANTONIO A good sharp fellow; I will send for him, and question him yourself.

LEONATO No, no, we will hold it as a dream till it appear itself; but I will acquaint my daughter withal, that she may be the better prepared for an answer, if peradventure 20 this be true. Go you and tell her of it.   [*Exit Antonio.*

Enter ATTENDANTS.²⁹

Cousins, you know what you have to do. — O, I cry you mercy, friend: go you with me and I will use your skill. — Good cousin, have a care this busy time.

SCENE 3.

Outside Leonato's house.[30]

Enter DON JOHN *and* CONRADE.

CONRADE   What the good-year, my lord?[31] Why are you thus out
of measure sad?

DON JOHN   There is no measure in the occasion that breeds, therefore the sadness is without limit.

CONRADE   You should hear reason.

DON JOHN   And when I have heard it, what blessing brings it?

CONRADE   If not a present remedy, at least a patient sufferance.

DON JOHN   I wonder that thou (being, as thou say'st thou art, born
under Saturn)[32] goest about to apply a moral medicine to
a mortifying mischief. I cannot hide what I am: I must be   10
sad when I have cause, and smile at no man's jests; eat
when I have stomach, and wait for no man's leisure; sleep
when I am drowsy, and tend on no man's business; laugh
when I am merry, and claw no man in his humour.[33]

CONRADE   Yea, but you must not make the full show of this till
you may do it without controlment. You have of late
stood out against your brother, and he hath ta'en you
newly into his grace, where it is impossible you should
take true root but by the fair weather that you make
yourself. It is needful that you frame the season for   20
your own harvest.

DON JOHN   I had rather be a canker in a hedge than a rose in his
grace; and it better fits my blood to be disdained of all,
than to fashion a carriage to rob love from any. In this
(though I cannot be said to be a flattering honest man),
it must not be denied but I am a plain-dealing villain. I
am trusted with a muzzle and enfranchised with a
clog:[34] therefore I have decreed not to sing in my cage.
If I had my mouth, I would bite; if I had my liberty, I
would do my liking; in the meantime, let me be that I   30
am, and seek not to alter me.

CONRADE   Can you make no use of your discontent?

DON JOHN I make all use of it, for I use it only. Who comes here?

Enter BORACHIO.

What news, Borachio?

BORACHIO I came yonder from a great supper. The Prince your brother is royally entertained by Leonato, and I can give you intelligence of an intended marriage.

DON JOHN Will it serve for any model to build mischief on? What is he for a fool that betroths himself to unquietness?

BORACHIO Marry, it is your brother's right hand.   40

DON JOHN Who, the most exquisite Claudio?

BORACHIO Even he.

DON JOHN A proper squire, and who, and who — which way looks he?

BORACHIO Marry, on Hero, the daughter and heir of Leonato.

DON JOHN A very forward March-chick! How came you to this?

BORACHIO Being entertained for a perfumer, as I was smoking a musty room, comes me the Prince and Claudio, hand in hand in sad conference.[35] I whipped me behind the arras, and there heard it agreed upon that the Prince 50 should woo Hero for himself, and, having obtained her, give her to Count Claudio.

DON JOHN Come, come, let us thither: this may prove food to my displeasure. That young start-up hath all the glory of my overthrow: if I can cross him any way, I bless myself every way. You are both sure, and will assist me?

CONRADE To the death, my lord.

DON JOHN Let us to the great supper. Their cheer is the greater that I am subdued; would the cook were o' my mind![36] Shall we go prove what's to be done?   60

BORACHIO We'll wait upon your lordship.

[Exeunt.

ACT 2, SCENE 1.

A hall in Leonato's house.[37]

Enter LEONATO, INNOGEN, ANTONIO,
HERO, BEATRICE *and a* KINSMAN.

LEONATO   Was not Count John here at supper?

ANTONIO   I saw him not.

BEATRICE   How tartly that gentleman looks. I never can see him
but I am heart-burned an hour after.

HERO   He is of a very melancholy disposition.

BEATRICE   He were an excellent man that were made just in the
mid-way between him and Benedick: the one is too
like an image and says nothing, and the other too like
my lady's eldest son, evermore tattling.

LEONATO   Then half Signior Benedick's tongue in Count John's   10
mouth, and half Count John's melancholy in Signior
Benedick's face —

BEATRICE   With a good leg and a good foot, uncle, and money
enough in his purse, such a man would win any
woman in the world — if a could get her good will.

LEONATO   By my troth, niece, thou wilt never get thee a husband, if thou be so shrewd of thy tongue.

ANTONIO   In faith, she's too curst.

BEATRICE   Too curst is more than curst. I shall lessen God's
sending that way, for it is said, 'God sends a curst cow   20
short horns', but to a cow too curst he sends none.[38]

LEONATO   So by being too curst, God will send you no horns?

BEATRICE   Just, if he send me no husband: for the which blessing
I am at him upon my knees every morning and
evening. Lord, I could not endure a husband with a
beard on his face; I had rather lie in the woollen.

LEONATO   You may light on a husband that hath no beard.

BEATRICE   What should I do with him? Dress him in my apparel
and make him my waiting-gentlewoman? He that
hath a beard is more than a youth; and he that hath   30
no beard is less than a man; and he that is more than a
youth is not for me, and he that is less than a man, I
am not for him. Therefore I will even take sixpence

in earnest of the bear'ard and lead his apes into hell.[39]

LEONATO   Well then, go you into hell.

BEATRICE   No, but to the gate, and there will the devil meet me
like an old cuckold with horns on his head, and say,
'Get you to heaven, Beatrice, get you to heaven;
here's no place for you maids.' So deliver I up my
apes, and away to Saint Peter: for the heavens, he   40
shows me where the bachelors sit, and there live we as
merry as the day is long.[40]

ANTONIO   [to Hero:] Well, niece, I trust you will be ruled by your
father.

BEATRICE   Yes, faith, it is my cousin's duty to make curtsy and say,
'Father, as it please you'; but yet for all that, cousin, let
him be a handsome fellow, or else make another
curtsy, and say, 'Father, as it please me.'

LEONATO   Well, niece, I hope to see you one day fitted with a
husband.   50

BEATRICE   Not till God make men of some other mettle than
earth. Would it not grieve a woman to be over-
mastered with a piece of valiant dust? To make an
account of her life to a clod of wayward marl? No,
uncle, I'll none: Adam's sons are my brethren, and truly
I hold it a sin to match in my kindred.[41]

LEONATO   Daughter, remember what I told you. If the Prince do
solicit you in that kind, you know your answer.

BEATRICE   The fault will be in the music, cousin, if you be not
wooed in good time. If the Prince be too important,   60
tell him there is measure in every thing, and so dance
out the answer.[42] For hear me, Hero: wooing, wedding,
and repenting, is as a Scotch jig, a measure, and a cinque-
pace: the first suit is hot and hasty like a Scotch jig, and
full as fantastical; the wedding mannerly-modest, as a
measure, full of state and ancientry; and then comes
Repentance, and with his bad legs falls into the cinque-
pace faster and faster, till he sink into his grave.

LEONATO   Cousin, you apprehend passing shrewdly.

BEATRICE   I have a good eye, uncle. I can see a church by daylight.   70

LEONATO   The revellers are entering, brother; make good room.

                    [Antonio moves aside, donning a mask.

Enter DON PEDRO, CLAUDIO, BENEDICK *and* BALTHASAR, *all masked,*
with a DRUMMER, *followed by* MARGARET, URSULA, DON JOHN, *and*
BORACHIO.[43] MUSICIANS *enter and play. The dance ensues.*

D. PEDRO	[*to Hero:*] Lady, will you walk a bout with your friend?
HERO	So you walk softly, and look sweetly, and say nothing, I am yours for the walk – and especially when I walk away.
D. PEDRO	With me in your company?
HERO	I may say so when I please.
D. PEDRO	And when please you to say so?
HERO	When I like your favour, for God defend the lute should be like the case! 80
D. PEDRO	My visor is Philemon's roof; within the house is Jove.
HERO	Why, then your visor should be thatched.
D. PEDRO	Speak low if you speak love.[44]

[*They move on.*

BALTH.	Well, I would you did like me.
MARGARET	So would not I for your own sake, for I have many ill qualities.
BALTH.	Which is one?
MARGARET	I say my prayers aloud.
BALTH.	I love you the better: the hearers may cry 'Amen'.
MARGARET	God match me with a good dancer.
BALTH.	Amen. 90
MARGARET	And God keep him out of my sight when the dance is done. Answer, clerk.
BALTH.	No more words; the clerk is answered.[45]

[*They move on.*

URSULA	I know you well enough: you are Signior Antonio.
ANTONIO	At a word, I am not.
URSULA	I know you by the waggling of your head.
ANTONIO	To tell you true, I counterfeit him.
URSULA	You could never do him so ill-well, unless you were the very man. Here's his dry hand up and down: you are he, you are he. 100
ANTONIO	At a word, I am not.
URSULA	Come, come, do you think I do not know you by your

excellent wit? Can virtue hide itself? Go to, mum, you
are he; graces will appear, and there's an end.

[They move on.

BEATRICE   Will you not tell me who told you so?

BENEDICK   No, you shall pardon me.

BEATRICE   Nor will you not tell me who you are?

BENEDICK   Not now.

BEATRICE   That I was disdainful, and that I had my good wit out
of the *Hundred Merry Tales*[46] – well, this was Signior   110
Benedick that said so.

BENEDICK   What's he?

BEATRICE   I am sure you know him well enough.

BENEDICK   Not I, believe me.

BEATRICE   Did he never make you laugh?

BENEDICK   I pray you, what is he?

BEATRICE   Why, he is the Prince's jester, a very dull Fool: only
his gift is in devising impossible slanders.[47] None but
libertines delight in him, and the commendation is not
in his wit but in his villainy, for he both pleases men   120
and angers them, and then they laugh at him and beat
him. I am sure he is in the fleet; I would he had
boarded me.[48]

BENEDICK   When I know the gentleman, I'll tell him what you
say.

BEATRICE   Do, do. He'll but break a comparison or two on me,
which peradventure, not marked or not laughed at,
strikes him into melancholy; and then there's a partridge
wing saved, for the Fool will eat no supper that night.
We must follow the leaders.   130

BENEDICK   In every good thing.

BEATRICE   Nay, if they lead to any ill, I will leave them at the next
turning.

*Music and dancing continue and conclude. Exeunt all (including
Don Pedro accompanying Leonato) except Don John,
Borachio and Claudio.*

DON JOHN   [*to Borachio:*] Sure, my brother is amorous on Hero,
and hath withdrawn her father to break with him about
it. The ladies follow her, and but one visor remains.

BORACHIO   And that is Claudio: I know him by his bearing.

DON JOHN   [*to Claudio:*] Are not you Signior Benedick?

CLAUDIO   You know me well; I am he.

DON JOHN   Signior, you are very near my brother in his love.[49] He   140
is enamoured on Hero. I pray you, dissuade him from
her: she is no equal for his birth. You may do the part
of an honest man in it.

CLAUDIO   How know you he loves her?

DON JOHN   I heard him swear his affection.

BORACHIO   So did I too, and he swore he would marry her tonight.

DON JOHN   [*to Borachio:*] Come, let us to the banquet.

[*Exeunt Don John and Borachio.*

CLAUDIO   Thus answer I in name of Benedick,
But hear these ill news with the ears of Claudio.
'Tis certain so: the Prince woos for himself.   150
Friendship is constant in all other things
Save in the office and affairs of love:
Therefore all hearts in love use their own tongues.
Let every eye negotiate for itself,
And trust no agent: for beauty is a witch
Against whose charms faith melteth into blood.
This is an accident of hourly proof,
Which I mistrusted not.[50] Farewell, therefore, Hero.

Enter BENEDICK, *unmasked.*

BENEDICK   Count Claudio?

CLAUDIO   Yea, the same.   160

BENEDICK   Come, will you go with me?

CLAUDIO   Whither?

BENEDICK   Even to the next willow, about your own business,
County. What fashion will you wear the garland of?
About your neck, like an usurer's chain? Or under
your arm, like a lieutenant's scarf? You must wear it
one way, for the Prince hath got your Hero.[51]

CLAUDIO   I wish him joy of her.

BENEDICK   Why, that's spoken like an honest drovier – so they
sell bullocks; but did you think the Prince would have   170
served you thus?

CLAUDIO   I pray you, leave me!   [*He hits Benedick.*

BENEDICK Ho, now you strike like the blind man: 'twas the boy
that stole your meat, and you'll beat the post.

CLAUDIO If it will not be, I'll leave you.   [Exit.

BENEDICK Alas, poor hurt fowl, now will he creep into sedges.
But, that my Lady Beatrice should know me, and not
know me. 'The Prince's Fool'! Ha, it may be I go under
that title because I am merry; yea, but so I am apt to do
myself wrong. I am not so reputed: it is the base (though 180
bitter) disposition of Beatrice, that puts the world into
her person, and so gives me out.⁵² Well, I'll be revenged
as I may.

Enter DON PEDRO, *followed by* LEONATO
and HERO, *who talk privately.*⁵³

D. PEDRO Now, signior, where's the Count? Did you see him?

BENEDICK Troth, my lord, I have played the part of Lady Fame. I
found him here as melancholy as a lodge in a warren.⁵⁴
I told him, and I think I told him true, that your Grace
had got the good will of this young lady, and I offered
him my company to a willow tree, either to make him
a garland, as being forsaken, or to bind him up a rod, 190
as being worthy to be whipped.

D. PEDRO 'To be whipped'? What's his fault?

BENEDICK The flat transgression of a schoolboy, who, being over-
joyed with finding a bird's-nest, shows it his companion,
and he steals it.

D. PEDRO Wilt thou make a trust a transgression? The transgression
is in the stealer.

BENEDICK Yet it had not been amiss the rod had been made, and
the garland too: for the garland he might have worn
himself, and the rod he might have bestowed on you, 200
who (as I take it) have stolen his bird's-nest.

D. PEDRO I will but teach them to sing, and restore them to the
owner.

BENEDICK If their singing answer your saying, by my faith you say
honestly.

D. PEDRO The Lady Beatrice hath a quarrel to you. The gentleman
that danced with her told her she is much wronged
by you.

BENEDICK O, she misused me past the endurance of a block: an oak
but with one green leaf on it would have answered her; 210
my very visor began to assume life and scold with her.
She told me, not thinking I had been myself, that I was
the Prince's jester, that I was duller than a great thaw;
huddling jest upon jest with such impossible conveyance
upon me, that I stood like a man at a mark, with a whole
army shooting at me.[55] She speaks poniards, and every
word stabs: if her breath were as terrible as her terminations, there were no living near her: she would infect to
the North Star.[56] I would not marry her, though she were
endowed with all that Adam had left him before he trans- 220
gressed. She would have made Hercules have turned spit,
yea, and have cleft his club to make the fire too. Come,
talk not of her. You shall find her the infernal Ate in
good apparel. I would to God some scholar would conjure her,[57] for certainly, while she is here, a man may live
as quiet in hell as in a sanctuary, and people sin upon
purpose because they would go thither, so indeed all
disquiet, horror and perturbation follows her.

Enter CLAUDIO *and* BEATRICE.

D. PEDRO Look, here she comes.
BENEDICK Will your Grace command me any service to the 230
world's end? I will go on the slightest errand now to
the Antipodes that you can devise to send me on: I
will fetch you a tooth-picker now from the furthest
inch of Asia, bring you the length of Prester John's
foot, fetch you a hair off the Great Cham's beard, do
you any embassage to the Pigmies, rather than hold
three words' conference with this harpy.[58] You have
no employment for me?
D. PEDRO None, but to desire your good company.
BENEDICK O God, sir, here's a dish I love not. I cannot endure 240
my Lady Tongue.   [*Exit.*
D. PEDRO Come, lady, come, you have lost the heart of Signior
Benedick.
BEATRICE Indeed my lord, he lent it me awhile, and I gave him
use for it: a double heart for his single one. Marry,

once before he won it of me with false dice, therefore
your Grace may well say I have lost it.[59]

D. PEDRO   You have put him down, lady, you have put him
down.

BEATRICE   So I would not he should do me, my lord, lest I should 250
prove the mother of fools. I have brought Count
Claudio, whom you sent me to seek.

D. PEDRO   Why, how now, Count: wherefore are you sad?

CLAUDIO   Not sad, my lord.

D. PEDRO   How then? Sick?

CLAUDIO   Neither, my lord.

BEATRICE   The Count is neither sad, nor sick, nor merry, nor
well; but civil Count — civil as an orange, and something of that jealous complexion.[60]

D. PEDRO   I'faith, lady, I think your blazon to be true; though I'll 260
be sworn, if he be so, his conceit is false. Here, Claudio,
I have wooed in thy name, and fair Hero is won; I have
broke with her father, and his good will obtained. Name
the day of marriage, and God give thee joy.

LEONATO   Count, take of me my daughter, and with her my
fortunes: his Grace hath made the match, and all grace
say 'Amen' to it.[61]

BEATRICE   Speak, Count, 'tis your cue.

CLAUDIO   Silence is the perfectest herald of joy: I were but little
happy, if I could say how much. [*To Hero:*] Lady, as 270
you are mine, I am yours; I give away myself for you,
and dote upon the exchange.

BEATRICE   Speak cousin, or, if you cannot, stop his mouth with a
kiss, and let not him speak neither. [*Hero kisses Claudio.*

D. PEDRO   In faith, lady, you have a merry heart.

BEATRICE   Yea, my lord, I thank it; poor Fool, it keeps on the
windy side of care.[62] My cousin tells him in his ear that
he is in her heart.

CLAUDIO   And so she doth, cousin.

BEATRICE   Good Lord, for alliance! Thus goes every one to the 280
world but I, and I am sun-burnt; I may sit in a corner
and cry 'Heigh-ho for a husband'.[63]

D. PEDRO   Lady Beatrice, I will get you one.

BEATRICE   I would rather have one of your father's getting: hath your Grace ne'er a brother like you? Your father got excellent husbands, if a maid could come by them.

D. PEDRO   Will you have *me*, lady?

BEATRICE   No my lord, unless I might have another for working-days: your Grace is too costly to wear every day. But I beseech your Grace, pardon me: I was born to speak 290 all mirth and no matter.

D. PEDRO   Your silence most offends me, and to be merry best becomes you, for out o' question you were born in a merry hour.

BEATRICE   No, sure, my lord, my mother cried; but then there was a star danced, and under that was I born.[64] – Cousins, God give you joy!

LEONATO   Niece, will you look to those things I told you of?

BEATRICE   I cry you mercy, uncle. – By your Grace's pardon.

[*Exit.*

D. PEDRO   By my troth, a pleasant-spirited lady.   300

LEONATO   There's little of the melancholy element[65] in her, my lord. She is never sad but when she sleeps, and not ever sad then: for I have heard my daughter say, she hath often dreamt of unhappiness and waked herself with laughing.

D. PEDRO   She cannot endure to hear tell of a husband.

LEONATO   O, by no means: she mocks all her wooers out of suit.

D. PEDRO   She were an excellent wife for Benedick.

LEONATO   O Lord, my lord, if they were but a week married, they would talk themselves mad.   310

D. PEDRO   Count Claudio, when mean you to go to church?

CLAUDIO   Tomorrow, my lord. Time goes on crutches till love have all his rites.

LEONATO   Not till Monday, my dear son, which is hence a just seven-night; and a time too brief too, to have all things answer my mind.

D. PEDRO   Come, you shake the head at so long a breathing, but I warrant thee, Claudio, the time shall not go dully by us. I will, in the interim, undertake one of Hercules' labours, which is, to bring Signior Benedick and the 320 Lady Beatrice into a mountain of affection, th'one with th'other. I would fain have it a match; and I doubt not

but to fashion it, if you three will but minister such
assistance as I shall give you direction.

LEONATO   My lord, I am for you, though it cost me ten nights'
watchings.

CLAUDIO   And I, my lord.

D. PEDRO   And you too, gentle Hero?

HERO   I will do any modest office, my lord, to help my cousin
to a good husband.   330

D. PEDRO   And Benedick is not the unhopefullest husband that I
know. Thus far can I praise him: he is of a noble strain,
of approved valour, and confirmed honesty. [*To Hero*:]
I will teach you how to humour your cousin, that she
shall fall in love with Benedick; [*to Leonato and
Claudio*:] and I, with your two helps, will so practise
on Benedick that, in despite of his quick wit and his
queasy stomach, he shall fall in love with Beatrice. If
we can do this, Cupid is no longer an archer: his glory
shall be ours, for we are the only love-gods. Go in   340
with me, and I will tell you my drift.

[*Exeunt.*

SCENE 2.

In Leonato's house.

Enter DON JOHN *and* BORACHIO.

DON JOHN   It is so; the Count Claudio shall marry the daughter of
Leonato.

BORACHIO   Yea, my lord, but I can cross it.

DON JOHN   Any bar, any cross, any impediment will be med'cinable
to me. I am sick in displeasure to him, and whatsoever
comes athwart his affection ranges evenly with mine.
How canst thou cross this marriage?

BORACHIO   Not honestly, my lord, but so covertly that no
dishonesty shall appear in me.

DON JOHN   Show me briefly how.   10

BORACHIO   I think I told your lordship, a year since, how much I
am in the favour of Margaret, the waiting gentlewoman
to Hero.

DON JOHN I remember.

BORACHIO I can, at any unseasonable instant of the night, appoint
her to look out at her lady's chamber-window.

DON JOHN What life is in that to be the death of this marriage?

BORACHIO The poison of that lies in you to temper. Go you to
the Prince your brother; spare not to tell him that he
hath wronged his honour in marrying the renowned 20
Claudio (whose estimation do you mightily hold up)
to a contaminated stale, such a one as Hero.

DON JOHN What proof shall I make of that?

BORACHIO Proof enough to misuse the Prince, to vex Claudio, to
undo Hero, and kill Leonato. Look you for any other
issue?

DON JOHN Only to despite them I will endeavour anything.

BORACHIO Go then, find me a meet hour to draw Don Pedro
and the Count Claudio alone, tell them that you
know that Hero loves me, intend a kind of zeal both 30
to the Prince and Claudio (as in love of your brother's
honour, who hath made this match, and his friend's
reputation, who is thus like to be cozened with the
semblance of a maid).[66] That you have discovered this,
they will scarcely believe without trial: offer them
instances, which shall bear no less likelihood than to see
me at her chamber-window, hear me call Margaret
Hero, hear Margaret term me Claudio;[67] and bring
them to see this the very night before the intended
wedding (for in the meantime I will so fashion the 40
matter that Hero shall be absent), and there shall appear
such seeming truth of Hero's disloyalty, that jealousy
shall be called assurance, and all the preparation over-
thrown.

DON JOHN Grow this to what adverse issue it can, I will put it in
practice. Be cunning in the working this, and thy fee is
a thousand ducats.

BORACHIO Be you constant in the accusation, and my cunning shall
not shame me.

DON JOHN I will presently go learn their day of marriage. [*Exeunt.* 50

SCENE 3.

Leonato's orchard.

Enter BENEDICK.

BENEDICK Boy!

Enter BOY.

BOY   Signior?

BENEDICK In my chamber-window lies a book: bring it hither to
me in the orchard.

BOY   I am here already, sir.[68]

BENEDICK I know that; but I would have thee hence, and here
again.   [*Exit boy.*
I do much wonder, that one man, seeing how much
another man is a fool when he dedicates his behaviours to
love, will, after he hath laughed at such shallow follies in 10
others, become the argument of his own scorn by falling
in love. And such a man is Claudio. I have known when
there was no music with him but the drum and the fife,
and now had he rather hear the tabor and the pipe.[69] I
have known when he would have walked ten mile afoot
to see a good armour, and now will he lie ten nights
awake carving the fashion of a new doublet. He was
wont to speak plain and to the purpose (like an honest
man and a soldier), and now is he turned orthography: his
words are a very fantastical banquet, just so many strange 20
dishes. May I be so converted, and see with these eyes? I
cannot tell; I think not. I will not be sworn but love may
transform me to an oyster; but I'll take my oath on it, till
he have made an oyster of me, he shall never make me
such a fool. One woman is fair, yet I am well; another is
wise, yet I am well; another virtuous, yet I am well; but
till all graces be in one woman, one woman shall not
come in my grace. Rich she shall be, that's certain; wise,
or I'll none; virtuous, or I'll never cheapen her; fair, or
I'll never look on her; mild, or come not near me; noble, 30
or not I for an angel;[70] of good discourse, an excellent

musician, and her hair shall be of what colour it please
God. – Ha! The Prince and Monsieur Love! I will hide
me in the arbour.   [*He hides.*

Enter DON PEDRO, LEONATO *and* CLAUDIO
followed by BALTHASAR *with a lute.*[71]

D. PEDRO   Come, shall we hear this music?
CLAUDIO   Yea, my good lord. How still the evening is,
           As hushed on purpose to grace harmony!
D. PEDRO   [*aside:*] See you where Benedick hath hid himself?
CLAUDIO   [*aside:*] O very well, my lord: the music ended,
           We'll fit the kid-fox with a pennyworth.[72]   40
D. PEDRO   Come, Balthasar, we'll hear that song again.
BALTH.   O good my lord, tax not so bad a voice
           To slander music any more than once.
D. PEDRO   It is the witness still of excellency,
           To put a strange face on his own perfection.[73]
           I pray thee sing, and let me woo no more.
BALTH.   Because you talk of wooing, I will sing:
           Since many a wooer doth commence his suit
           To her he thinks not worthy, yet he woos,
           Yet will he swear he loves.
D. PEDRO   Nay, pray thee, come,   50
           Or, if thou wilt hold longer argument,
           Do it in notes.
BALTH.   Note this before my notes:
           There's not a note of mine that's worth the noting.
D. PEDRO   Why, these are very crotchets that he speaks –
           Note notes, forsooth, and nothing![74]   [*Balthasar plays.*
BENEDICK   Now, divine air! Now is his soul ravished. Is it not
           strange that sheeps' guts should hale souls out of men's
           bodies? Well, a horn for my money, when all's done.[75]
BALTH.   [*singing:*]
                   Sigh no more, ladies, sigh no more;
                     Men were deceivers ever: 60
                   One foot in sea, and one on shore,
                     To one thing constant never.
                       Then sigh not so, but let them go,
                         And be you blithe and bonny,

> Converting all your sounds of woe
> Into 'Hey nonny, nonny'.

> Sing no more ditties, sing no moe
>   Of dumps so dull and heavy;
> The fraud of men was ever so,
>   Since summer first was leavy.   70
>   Then sigh not so, but let them go,
>   And be you blithe and bonny,
>   Converting all your sounds of woe
>   Into 'Hey nonny, nonny'.

D. PEDRO   By my troth, a good song.

BALTH.   And an ill singer, my lord.

D. PEDRO   Ha, no, no, faith: thou sing'st well enough for a shift.
               [He talks quietly with Claudio and Leonato.

BENEDICK   *[aside:]* And he had been a dog that should have howled
               thus, they would have hanged him. And I pray God his
               bad voice bode no mischief; I had as lief have heard the 80
               night-raven, come what plague could have come after it.

D. PEDRO   Yea, marry. — Dost thou hear, Balthasar? I pray thee get
               us some excellent music: for tomorrow night we would
               have it at the Lady Hero's chamber-window.

BALTH.   The best I can, my lord.

D. PEDRO   Do so; farewell.   *[Exit Balthasar.*
               Come hither, Leonato. What was it you told me of to-
               day? That your niece Beatrice was in love with Signior
               Benedick?

CLAUDIO   *[aside to Don Pedro, noting that Benedick is still eaves-
               dropping:]* O ay, stalk on, stalk on: the fowl sits. *[Aloud:]* 90
               I did never think that lady would have loved any man.

LEONATO   No, nor I neither; but most wonderful that she should
               so dote on Signior Benedick, whom she hath in all
               outward behaviours seemed ever to abhor.

BENEDICK   *[aside:]* Is't possible? Sits the wind in that corner?[76]

LEONATO   By my troth, my lord, I cannot tell what to think of it,
               but that she loves him with an enraged affection. It is
               past the infinite of thought.[77]

D. PEDRO   May be she doth but counterfeit.

CLAUDIO   Faith, like enough.   100

LEONATO   O God! Counterfeit? There was never counterfeit of
            passion came so near the life of passion as she dis-
            covers it.
D. PEDRO   Why, what effects of passion shows she?
CLAUDIO   [*aside:*] Bait the hook well: this fish will bite.
LEONATO   What effects, my lord? She will sit you – [*to Claudio:*]
            you heard my daughter tell you how.
CLAUDIO   She did, indeed.
D. PEDRO   How, how, I pray you? You amaze me. I would have
            thought her spirit had been invincible against all assaults   110
            of affection.
LEONATO   I would have sworn it had, my lord; especially against
            Benedick.
BENEDICK   [*aside:*] I should think this a gull, but that the white-
            bearded fellow speaks it: knavery cannot, sure, hide
            himself in such reverence.
CLAUDIO   [*aside to Pedro:*] He hath ta'en th'infection; hold it up.
D. PEDRO   Hath she made her affection known to Benedick?
LEONATO   No, and swears she never will; that's her torment.
CLAUDIO   'Tis true indeed, so your daughter says. 'Shall I,' says   120
            she, 'that have so oft encountered him with scorn, write
            to him that I love him?'
LEONATO   This says she now, when she is beginning to write to
            him, for she'll be up twenty times a night, and there
            will she sit in her smock till she have writ a sheet of
            paper: my daughter tells us all.
CLAUDIO   Now you talk of a sheet of paper, I remember a pretty
            jest your daughter told us of.
LEONATO   O, when she had writ it, and was reading it over, she
            found 'Benedick' and 'Beatrice' between the sheet?   130
CLAUDIO   That.
LEONATO   O, she tore the letter into a thousand half-pence; railed
            at herself that she should be so immodest to write to
            one that she knew would flout her. 'I measure him',
            says she, 'by my own spirit, for I should flout him if he
            writ to me; yea, though I love him, I should.'
CLAUDIO   Then down upon her knees she falls, weeps, sobs, beats
            her heart, tears her hair, prays, curses: 'O sweet Bene-
            dick! God give me patience!'

LEONATO   She doth indeed: my daughter says so; and the ecstasy   140
          hath so much overborne her, that my daughter is some-
          time afeard she will do a desperate outrage to herself. It
          is very true.

D. PEDRO It were good that Benedick knew of it by some other,
          if she will not discover it.

CLAUDIO   To what end? He would make but a sport of it, and
          torment the poor lady worse.

D. PEDRO And he should, it were an alms to hang him. She's an
          excellent sweet lady, and (out of all suspicion) she is vir-
          tuous.   150

CLAUDIO   And she is exceeding wise.

D. PEDRO In everything but in loving Benedick.

LEONATO   O my lord, wisdom and blood combating in so tender
          a body, we have ten proofs to one that blood hath the
          victory. I am sorry for her, as I have just cause, being
          her uncle and her guardian.

D. PEDRO I would she had bestowed this dotage on me. I would
          have daffed all other respects, and made her half my-
          self. I pray you tell Benedick of it, and hear what a
          will say.   160

LEONATO   Were it good, think you?

CLAUDIO   Hero thinks surely she will die, for she says she will die
          if he love her not, and she will die ere she make her
          love known, and she will die if he woo her, rather than
          she will bate one breath of her accustomed crossness.

D. PEDRO She doth well. If she should make tender of her love,
          'tis very possible he'll scorn it, for the man (as you
          know all) hath a contemptible spirit.

CLAUDIO   He is a very proper man.

D. PEDRO He hath indeed a good outward happiness.   170

CLAUDIO   Before God, and in my mind, very wise.

D. PEDRO He doth indeed show some sparks that are like wit.

CLAUDIO   And I take him to be valiant.

D. PEDRO As Hector, I assure you; and in the managing of
          quarrels you may say he is wise, for either he avoids
          them with great discretion, or undertakes them with a
          most Christian-like fear.

LEONATO   If he do fear God, a must necessarily keep peace; if he

break the peace, he ought to enter into a quarrel with
fear and trembling.⁷⁸   180

D. PEDRO And so will he do: for the man doth fear God, how-
soever it seems not in him by some large jests he will
make. Well, I am sorry for your niece. Shall we go
seek Benedick, and tell him of her love?

CLAUDIO Never tell him, my lord. Let her wear it out with good
counsel.

LEONATO Nay, that's impossible; she may wear her heart out first.

D. PEDRO Well, we will hear further of it by your daughter. Let
it cool the while. I love Benedick well, and I could
wish he would modestly examine himself, to see how 190
much he is unworthy so good a lady.

LEONATO My lord, will you walk? Dinner is ready.

                    [*They walk away from the arbour.*

CLAUDIO [*aside:*] If he do not dote on her upon this, I will never
trust my expectation.

D. PEDRO [*aside:*] Let there be the same net spread for her, and that
must your daughter and her gentlewomen carry. The
sport will be, when they hold one an opinion of
another's dotage, and no such matter.⁷⁹ That's the scene
that I would see, which will be merely a dumb-show.
Let us send her to call him in to dinner.   200

                    [*Exeunt Don Pedro, Claudio and Leonato.*
                    Benedick emerges.

BENEDICK This can be no trick: the conference was sadly borne;
they have the truth of this from Hero; they seem to
pity the lady. It seems her affections have their full
bent. Love me? Why, it must be requited. I hear how I
am censured: they say I will bear myself proudly, if I
perceive the love come from her; they say too that she
will rather die than give any sign of affection. I did
never think to marry. I must not seem proud: happy
are they that hear their detractions, and can put them
to mending. They say the lady is fair: 'tis a truth, I can 210
bear them witness; and virtuous: 'tis so, I cannot reprove it; and wise, but for loving me: by my troth, it is
no addition to her wit, nor no great argument of her
folly, for I will be horribly in love with her. I may

2, 3   MUCH ADO ABOUT NOTHING   59

chance have some odd quirks and remnants of wit broken on me, because I have railed so long against marriage: but doth not the appetite alter? A man loves the meat in his youth that he cannot endure in his age. Shall quips and sentences and these paper bullets of the brain awe a man from the career of his humour? No; 220 the world must be peopled. When I said I would die a bachelor, I did not think I should live till I were married.

Enter BEATRICE.

Here comes Beatrice. By this day, she's a fair lady. I do spy some marks of love in her.

BEATRICE   Against my will, I am sent to bid you come in to dinner.

BENEDICK   Fair Beatrice, I thank you for your pains.

BEATRICE   I took no more pains for those thanks than you take pains to thank me. If it had been painful, I would not 230 have come.

BENEDICK   You take pleasure then in the message.

BEATRICE   Yea, just so much as you may take upon a knife's point, and choke a daw withal. You have no stomach, signior? Fare you well. [80]   [*Exit.*

BENEDICK   Ha! 'Against my will, I am sent to bid you come in to dinner': there's a double meaning in that. 'I took no more pains for those thanks than you took pains to thank me': that's as much as to say, 'Any pains that I take for you is as easy as thanks'. If I do not take pity of 240 her, I am a villain; if I do not love her, I am a Jew. I will go get her picture. [81]   [*Exit.*

ACT 3, SCENE I.

The orchard.

Enter HERO, MARGARET, *and* URSULA.

HERO   Good Margaret, run thee to the parlour:
              There shalt thou find my cousin Beatrice
              Proposing with the Prince and Claudio.
              Whisper her ear, and tell her I and Ursley[82]
              Walk in the orchard, and our whole discourse
              Is all of her. Say that thou overheard'st us,
              And bid her steal into the pleachèd bower
              Where honeysuckles, ripened by the sun,
              Forbid the sun to enter, like favourites,
              Made proud by princes, that advance their pride   10
              Against that power that bred it. There will she hide her,
              To listen our propose. This is thy office;
              Bear thee well in it, and leave us alone.
MARGARET I'll make her come, I warrant you, presently.

                                                            [*Exit.*

HERO   Now, Ursula, when Beatrice doth come,
              As we do trace this alley up and down,
              Our talk must only be of Benedick.
              When I do name him, let it be thy part
              To praise him more than ever man did merit;
              My talk to thee must be how Benedick   20
              Is sick in love with Beatrice. Of this matter
              Is little Cupid's crafty arrow made,
              That only wounds by hearsay.

          Enter BEATRICE *stealthily. She hides in the arbour.*

                                        Now begin,
              For look where Beatrice, like a lapwing, runs
              Close by the ground, to hear our conference.
URSULA   The pleasant'st angling is to see the fish
              Cut with her golden oars the silver stream
              And greedily devour the treacherous bait:
              So angle we for Beatrice, who, even now,

Is couchèd in the woodbine coverture.   30
Fear you not my part of the dialogue.

HERO   Then go we near her, that her ear lose nothing
Of the false sweet bait that we lay for it.

        [They approach the arbour.

No, truly, Ursula, she is too disdainful:
I know her spirits are as coy and wild
As haggards of the rock.

URSULA   But are you sure
That Benedick loves Beatrice so entirely?

HERO   So says the Prince, and my new-trothèd lord.

URSULA   And did they bid you tell her of it, madam?

HERO   They did entreat me to acquaint her of it;   40
But I persuaded them, if they loved Benedick,
To wish him wrestle with affection,[83]
And never to let Beatrice know of it.

URSULA   Why did you so? Doth not the gentleman
Deserve as full as fortunate a bed
As ever Beatrice shall couch upon?

HERO   O god of love! I know he doth deserve
As much as may be yielded to a man;
But nature never framed a woman's heart
Of prouder stuff than that of Beatrice.   50
Disdain and scorn ride sparkling in her eyes,
Misprizing what they look on, and her wit
Values itself so highly that to her
All matter else seems weak: she cannot love,
Nor take no shape nor project of affection,[84]
She is so self-endeared.

URSULA   Sure, I think so;
And therefore certainly it were not good
She knew his love, lest she'll make sport at it.

HERO   Why, you speak truth. I never yet saw man,
How wise, how noble, young, how rarely featured,   60
But she would spell him backward: if fair-faced,
She would swear the gentleman should be her sister;
If black, why nature, drawing of an antic,
Made a foul blot; if tall, a lance ill-headed;
If low, an agate very vildly cut;

If speaking, why, a vane blown with all winds;
If silent, why, a block movèd with none.
So turns she every man the wrong side out,
And never gives to truth and virtue that
Which simpleness and merit purchaseth.   70

URSULA Sure, sure, such carping is not cómmendable.

HERO No, nor to be so odd and from all fashions,
As Beatrice is, cannot be cómmendable.
But who dare tell her so? If I should speak,
She would mock me into air; O, she would laugh me
Out of myself, press me to death with wit.
Therefore let Benedick, like covered fire,
Consume away in sighs, waste inwardly:[85]
It were a better death than die with mocks,
Which is as bad as die with tickling.   80

URSULA Yet tell her of it, hear what she will say.

HERO No, rather I will go to Benedick,
And counsel him to fight against his passion;
And, truly, I'll devise some honest slanders
To stain my cousin with. One doth not know
How much an ill word may empoison liking.

URSULA O, do not do your cousin such a wrong.
She cannot be so much without true judgement,
Having so swift and excellent a wit,
As she is prized to have, as to refuse   90
So rare a gentleman as Signior Benedick.

HERO He is the only man of Italy,
Always excepted my dear Claudio.

URSULA I pray you be not angry with me, madam,
Speaking my fancy: Signior Benedick,
For shape, for bearing, argument and valour,
Goes foremost in report through Italy.

HERO Indeed, he hath an excellent good name.

URSULA His excellence did earn it, ere he had it.
When are you married, madam?   100

HERO Why, every day, tomorrow![86] Come, go in:
I'll show thee some attires, and have thy counsel
Which is the best to furnish me tomorrow.

URSULA   [*aside:*] She's limed, I warrant you:[87] we have caught
                                                 her, madam.

HERO   [*aside:*] If it prove so, then loving goes by haps.
           Some Cupid kills with arrows, some with traps.
                                                 [*Exeunt.*

BEATRICE   [*emerging from the arbour:*]
               What fire is in mine ears? Can this be true?
                   Stand I condemned for pride and scorn so much?
               Contempt, farewell! And maiden pride, adieu!
                   No glory lives behind the back of such.   110
               And, Benedick, love on; I will requite thee,
                   Taming my wild heart to thy loving hand.
               If thou dost love, my kindness shall incite thee
                   To bind our loves up in a holy band:
               For others say thou dost deserve, and I
               Believe it better than reportingly.   [*Exit.*

SCENE 2.

In Leonato's house.

Enter DON PEDRO, CLAUDIO, BENEDICK *and* LEONATO.

D. PEDRO   I do but stay till your marriage be consummate, and
           then go I toward Arragon.

CLAUDIO   I'll bring you thither, my lord, if you'll vouchsafe me.

D. PEDRO   Nay, that would be as great a soil in the new gloss of
           your marriage, as to show a child his new coat and
           forbid him to wear it. I will only be bold with
           Benedick for his company, for, from the crown of his
           head to the sole of his foot, he is all mirth. He hath
           twice or thrice cut Cupid's bow-string, and the little
           hangman dare not shoot at him. He hath a heart as   10
           sound as a bell, and his tongue is the clapper: for what
           his heart thinks, his tongue speaks.

BENEDICK   Gallants, I am not as I have been.

LEONATO   So say I. Methinks you are sadder.

CLAUDIO   I hope he be in love.

D. PEDRO   Hang him, truant! There's no true drop of blood in him to be truly touched with love. If he be sad, he wants money.

BENEDICK I have the toothache.

D. PEDRO Draw it.   20

BENEDICK Hang it!

CLAUDIO You must hang it first, and draw it afterwards.

D. PEDRO What? Sigh for the toothache –

LEONATO Where is but a humour or a worm?

BENEDICK Well, every one can master a grief but he that has it.[88]

CLAUDIO [to Don Pedro and Leonato:] Yet say I, he is in love.

D. PEDRO There is no appearance of fancy in him, unless it be a fancy that he hath to strange disguises: as, to be a Dutchman today, a Frenchman tomorrow, or in the shape of two countries at once, as a German from the   30 waist downward, all slops, and a Spaniard from the hip upward, no doublet.[89] Unless he have a fancy to this foolery, as it appears he hath, he is no fool for fancy, as you would have it appear he is.

CLAUDIO If he be not in love with some woman, there is no believing old signs. A brushes his hat a mornings: what should that bode?

D. PEDRO Hath any man seen him at the barber's?

CLAUDIO No, but the barber's man hath been seen with him, and the old ornament of his cheek hath already stuffed   40 tennis-balls.[90]

LEONATO Indeed, he looks younger than he did, by the loss of a beard.

D. PEDRO Nay, a rubs himself with civet; can you smell him out by that?

CLAUDIO That's as much as to say, 'The sweet youth's in love.'

D. PEDRO The greatest note of it is his melancholy.

CLAUDIO And when was he wont to wash his face?

D. PEDRO Yea, or to paint himself? For the which, I hear what they say of him.   50

CLAUDIO Nay, but his jesting spirit, which is now crept into a lute-string and now governed by stops.[91]

D. PEDRO Indeed, that tells a heavy tale for him. Conclude, conclude, he is in love.

CLAUDIO Nay, but I know who loves him.

D. PEDRO   That would I know too. I warrant, one that knows
           him not.

CLAUDIO   Yes, and his ill conditions; and in despite of all, dies for
           him.

D. PEDRO   She shall be buried with her face upwards.[92]   60

BENEDICK   Yet is this no charm for the toothache. Old signior,
           walk aside with me. I have studied eight or nine wise
           words to speak to you, which these hobby-horses must
           not hear.   [*Exeunt Benedick and Leonato.*

D. PEDRO   For my life, to break with him about Beatrice.[93]

CLAUDIO   'Tis even so. Hero and Margaret have by this played
           their parts with Beatrice, and then the two bears will
           not bite one another when they meet.

                         Enter DON JOHN.

DON JOHN   My lord and brother, God save you.

D. PEDRO   Good-den, brother.   70

DON JOHN   If your leisure served, I would speak with you.

D. PEDRO   In private?

DON JOHN   If it please you; yet Count Claudio may hear, for what
           I would speak of concerns him.

CLAUDIO   What's the matter?

DON JOHN   Means your lordship to be married tomorrow?

D. PEDRO   You know he does.

DON JOHN   I know not that, when he knows what I know.

CLAUDIO   If there be any impediment, I pray you discover it.

DON JOHN   You may think I love you not; let that appear here-   80
           after, and aim better at me by that I now will manifest:
           for my brother (I think he holds you well, and in
           dearness of heart) hath holp to effect your ensuing
           marriage: surely, suit ill spent, and labour ill bestowed.

D. PEDRO   Why, what's the matter?

DON JOHN   I came hither to tell you, and, circumstances shortened
           (for she has been too long a-talking of), the lady is dis-
           loyal.

CLAUDIO   Who, Hero?

DON JOHN   Even she — Leonato's Hero, your Hero, every man's   90
           Hero.

CLAUDIO   Disloyal?

DON JOHN The word is too good to paint out her wickedness. I
could say she were worse; think you of a worse title, and
I will fit her to it. Wonder not till further warrant: go but
with me tonight, you shall see her chamber-window
entered, even the night before her wedding-day. If you
love her then, tomorrow wed her;[94] but it would better
fit your honour to change your mind.

CLAUDIO   May this be so?   100

D. PEDRO   I will not think it.

DON JOHN   If you dare not trust that you see, confess not that you
know. If you will follow me, I will show you enough;
and when you have seen more and heard more,
proceed accordingly.

CLAUDIO   If I see anything tonight why I should not marry her,
tomorrow, in the congregation, where I should wed,
there will I shame her.

D. PEDRO   And as I wooed for thee to obtain her, I will join with
thee to disgrace her.   110

DON JOHN   I will disparage her no farther till you are my wit-
nesses. Bear it coldly but till midnight, and let the issue
show itself.

D. PEDRO   O day untowardly turned!

CLAUDIO   O mischief strangely thwarting!

DON JOHN   O plague right well prevented! So will you say, when
you have seen the sequel.   [*Exeunt.*

SCENE 3.

Night. A street in Messina. In the centre, a church porch.

Enter DOGBERRY (*Chief Constable*), VERGES (*the Headborough*)
and several WATCHMEN.[95]

DOGBERRY   Are you good men and true?

VERGES   Yea, or else it were pity but they should suffer salvation,
body and soul.[96]

DOGBERRY   Nay, that were a punishment too good for them, if

they should have any allegiance in them, being chosen
for the Prince's watch.

VERGES   Well, give them their charge, neighbour Dogberry.

DOGBERRY First, who think you the most desertless man to be
constable?[97]

WATCH. 1 Hugh Oatcake, sir, or George Seacoal, for they can 10
write and read.

DOGBERRY Come hither, neighbour Seacoal. God hath blessed you
with a good name.[98] To be a well-favoured man is the
gift of fortune, but to write and read comes by nature.

WATCH. 2 Both which, Master Constable —

DOGBERRY You have: I knew it would be your answer. Well, for
your favour, sir, why, give God thanks, and make no
boast of it; and for your writing and reading, let that
appear when there is no need of such vanity. You are
thought here to be the most senseless and fit man for 20
the constable of the watch: therefore bear you the
lanthorn. This is your charge: you shall comprehend
all vagrom men; you are to bid any man stand, in the
Prince's name.

WATCH. 2 How if a will not stand?

DOGBERRY Why then take no note of him, but let him go, and
presently call the rest of the watch together, and thank
God you are rid of a knave.

VERGES   If he will not stand when he is bidden, he is none of
the Prince's subjects.   30

DOGBERRY True, and they are to meddle with none but the
Prince's subjects. — You shall also make no noise in the
streets: for, for the watch to babble and to talk, is most
tolerable and not to be endured.

WATCH. 2 We will rather sleep than talk: we know what belongs
to a watch.

DOGBERRY Why, you speak like an ancient and most quiet watchman, for I cannot see how sleeping should offend; only
have a care that your bills be not stolen. Well, you are
to call at all the ale-houses, and bid those that are 40
drunk get them to bed.

WATCH. 2 How if they will not?

DOGBERRY Why then, let them alone till they are sober. If they make you not then the better answer, you may say they are not the men you took them for.

WATCH. 2 Well, sir.

DOGBERRY If you meet a thief, you may suspect him, by virtue of your office, to be no true man; and, for such kind of men, the less you meddle or make with them, why, the more is for your honesty.   50

WATCH. 2 If we know him to be a thief, shall we not lay hands on him?

DOGBERRY Truly, by your office you may, but I think they that touch pitch will be defiled.[99] The most peaceable way for you, if you do take a thief, is to let him show himself what he is, and steal out of your company.

VERGES You have been always called a merciful man, partner.

DOGBERRY Truly, I would not hang a dog by my will, much more a man who hath any honesty in him.

VERGES If you hear a child cry in the night, you must call to   60 the nurse and bid her still it.

WATCH. 2 How if the nurse be asleep and will not hear us?

DOGBERRY Why then, depart in peace, and let the child wake her with crying; for the ewe that will not hear her lamb when it baas will never answer a calf when he bleats.

VERGES 'Tis very true.

DOGBERRY This is the end of the charge: you, constable, are to present the Prince's own person. If you meet the Prince in the night, you may stay him.

VERGES Nay, birlady, that I think a cannot.   70

DOGBERRY Five shillings to one on't with any man that knows the statutes, he may stay him; marry, not without the Prince be willing, for indeed the watch ought to offend no man, and it is an offence to stay a man against his will.

VERGES Birlady, I think it be so.

DOGBERRY Ha ah ha! Well, masters, good night. And there be any matter of weight chances, call up me.[100] Keep your fellows' counsels and your own, and good night. Come, neighbour.   [*They walk away.* 80

WATCH. 2 Well, masters, we hear our charge. Let us go sit here
upon the church-bench till two, and then all to bed.

[They enter the porch and sit.

DOGBERRY *[turns.]* One word more, honest neighbours. I pray you,
watch about Signior Leonato's door, for, the wedding
being there tomorrow, there is a great coil tonight.
Adieu; be vigitant, I beseech you.

[Exeunt Dogberry and Verges.

Enter BORACHIO *(drunk), followed by* CONRADE.

BORACHIO What, Conrade!

WATCH. 2 *[aside to the other watchmen:]* Peace, stir not.

BORACHIO Conrade, I say!

CONRADE Here, man, I am at thy elbow.   90

BORACHIO Mass, and my elbow itched: I thought there would a
scab follow.

CONRADE I will owe thee an answer for that; and now forward
with thy tale.

BORACHIO Stand thee close then under this pent-house, for it
drizzles rain, and I will, like a true drunkard, utter all
to thee.   *[They stand beneath the eaves of the porch.*

WATCH. 2 *[aside:]* Some treason, masters; yet stand close.

BORACHIO Therefore know, I have earned of Don John a thousand
ducats.   100

CONRADE Is it possible that any villainy should be so dear?

BORACHIO Thou shouldst rather ask if it were possible any villainy
should be so rich, for when rich villains have need of
poor ones, poor ones may make what price they will.

CONRADE I wonder at it.

BORACHIO That shows thou art unconfirmed. Thou knowest that
the fashion of a doublet, or a hat, or a cloak, is nothing
to a man.[101]

CONRADE Yes: it is apparel.

BORACHIO I mean the fashion.   110

CONRADE Yes, the fashion is the fashion.

BORACHIO Tush, I may as well say the fool's the fool. But seest
thou not what a deformed thief this fashion is?

WATCH. 2 *[aside:]* I know that Deformed: a has been a vile thief

this seven year; a goes up and down like a gentleman. I
remember his name.

BORACHIO Didst thou not hear somebody?

CONRADE No, 'twas the vane on the house.

BORACHIO Seest thou not, I say, what a deformed thief this fashion
is, how giddily a turns about all the hot-bloods between   120
fourteen and five-and-thirty, sometimes fashioning
them like Pharaoh's soldiers in the reechy painting,
sometime like god Bel's priests in the old church
window, sometime like the shaven Hercules in the
smirched worm-eaten tapestry, where his cod-piece
seems as massy as his club?[102]

CONRADE All this I see, and I see that the fashion wears out more
apparel than the man; but art not thou thyself giddy
with the fashion too, that thou hast shifted out of thy
tale into telling me of the fashion?   130

BORACHIO Not so neither; but know that I have tonight wooed
Margaret, the Lady Hero's gentlewoman, by the name
of Hero. She leans me out at her mistress' chamber-
window, bids me a thousand times good night. I tell
this tale vildly; I should first tell thee how the Prince,
Claudio and my master, planted and placed and possessed by my master Don John, saw afar off in the
orchard this amiable encounter.

CONRADE And thought they Margaret was Hero?

BORACHIO Two of them did, the Prince and Claudio; but the   140
devil, my master, knew she was Margaret; and partly
by his oaths, which first possessed them, partly by the
dark night, which did deceive them, but chiefly by my
villainy, which did confirm any slander that Don John
had made, away went Claudio enraged, swore he
would meet her as he was appointed next morning at
the temple, and there, before the whole congregation,
shame her with what he saw o'er-night, and send her
home again without a husband.   [*The watchmen emerge.*

WATCH. 2 We charge you in the Prince's name, stand![103]   150

WATCH. 1 Call up the right Master Constable. We have here re-
covered the most dangerous piece of lechery that ever
was known in the commonwealth.

WATCH. 2 And one Deformed is one of them: I know him, a wears
a lock.

CONRADE Masters, masters.

WATCH. 1 You'll be made bring Deformed forth, I warrant you.

CONRADE Masters —

WATCH. 2 Never speak, we charge you. Let us obey you to go
with us.[104]   160

BORACHIO [to Conrade:] We are like to prove a goodly commodity,
being taken up of these men's bills.

CONRADE A commodity in question, I warrant you.[105] — Come,
we'll obey you.   [Exeunt.

SCENE 4.

A room in Leonato's house.

Enter HERO, MARGARET *and* URSULA.

HERO Good Ursula, wake my cousin Beatrice, and desire her
to rise.

URSULA I will, lady.

HERO And bid her come hither.

URSULA Well.   [Exit.

MARGARET Troth, I think your other rebato were better.

HERO No, pray thee, good Meg, I'll wear this.

MARGARET By my troth, 's not so good, and I warrant your cousin
will say so.

HERO My cousin's a fool, and thou art another. I'll wear none 10
but this.

MARGARET I like the new tire within excellently, if the hair were a
thought browner; and your gown's a most rare fashion,
i'faith. I saw the Duchess of Millaine's gown that they
praise so —

HERO O, that exceeds, they say.

MARGARET By my troth, 's but a night-gown in respect of yours —
cloth o' gold and cuts, and laced with silver, set with
pearls, down sleeves, side-sleeves, and skirts round under-
borne with a bluish tinsel[106] — but, for a fine, quaint, 20
graceful and excellent fashion, yours is worth ten on't.

HERO   God give me joy to wear it, for my heart is exceeding
            heavy.

MARGARET   'Twill be heavier soon by the weight of a man.

HERO   Fie upon thee, art not ashamed?

MARGARET   Of what, lady? Of speaking honourably? Is not marriage
            honourable in a beggar? Is not your lord honourable
            without marriage? I think you would have me say,
            'saving your reverence, a husband'. And bad thinking
            do not wrest true speaking, I'll offend nobody: is there   30
            any harm in 'the heavier for a husband'? None, I think,
            and it be the right husband and the right wife, other-
            wise 'tis light and not heavy: ask my Lady Beatrice else.
            Here she comes.

                    Enter BEATRICE.

HERO   Good morrow, coz.

BEATRICE   Good morrow, sweet Hero.

HERO   Why, how now? Do you speak in the sick tune?

BEATRICE   I am out of all other tune, methinks.

MARGARET   Clap's into 'Light o' Love' (that goes without a burden):
            do you sing it, and I'll dance it.   40

BEATRICE   Ye light o' love with your heels: then if your husband
            have stables enough, you'll see he shall lack no barns.[107]

MARGARET   O illegitimate construction! I scorn that with my heels.

BEATRICE   'Tis almost five o'clock, cousin; 'tis time you were
            ready. By my troth, I am exceeding ill; hey-ho!

MARGARET   For a hawk, a horse, or a husband?

BEATRICE   For the letter that begins them all, H.

MARGARET   Well, and you be not turned Turk, there's no more
            sailing by the star.[108]

BEATRICE   What means the fool, trow?   50

MARGARET   Nothing, I; but God send every one their heart's desire.

HERO   These gloves the Count sent me, they are an excellent
            perfume.

BEATRICE   I am stuffed, cousin: I cannot smell.

MARGARET   A maid and stuffed! There's goodly catching of cold.

BEATRICE   O God help me, God help me, how long have you
            professed apprehension?

MARGARET   Ever since you left it.[109] Doth not my wit become me
            rarely?

BEATRICE   It is not seen enough; you should wear it in your cap. 60
            By my troth I am sick.

MARGARET   Get you some of this distilled *Carduus benedictus*, and lay
            it to your heart: it is the only thing for a qualm.[110]

HERO   There thou prick'st her with a thistle.

BEATRICE   *Benedictus*! Why *benedictus*? You have some moral in
            this *benedictus*.

MARGARET   Moral? No, by my troth, I have no moral meaning; I
            meant plain holy thistle. You may think perchance that
            I think you are in love; nay, birlady, I am not such a
            fool to think what I list, nor I list not to think what I 70
            can, nor indeed I cannot think, if I would think my
            heart out of thinking, that you are in love, or that you
            will be in love, or that you can be in love; yet Benedick
            was such another, and now is he become a man. He
            swore he would never marry, and yet now, in despite of
            his heart, he eats his meat without grudging;[111] and how
            you may be converted I know not, but methinks you
            look with your eyes as other women do.

BEATRICE   What pace is this that thy tongue keeps?

MARGARET   Not a false gallop.[112]   80

                        Enter URSULA.

URSULA   Madam, withdraw. The Prince, the Count, Signior
            Benedick, Don John and all the gallants of the town
            are come to fetch you to church.

HERO   Help to dress me, good coz, good Meg, good Ursula.
                                                        [*Exeunt.*

                        SCENE 5.

                    At Leonato's house.

            Enter LEONATO, DOGBERRY *and* VERGES.

LEONATO   What would you with me, honest neighbour?

DOGBERRY   Marry, sir, I would have some confidence with you,
            that decerns you nearly.[113]

LEONATO   Brief, I pray you, for you see it is a busy time with me.

DOGBERRY   Marry, this it is, sir.

VERGES   Yes, in truth it is, sir.

LEONATO   What is it, my good friends?

DOGBERRY Goodman Verges, sir, speaks a little off the matter; an
          old man, sir, and his wits are not so blunt as, God help,
          I would desire they were, but, in faith, honest as the   10
          skin between his brows.

VERGES   Yes, I thank God, I am as honest as any man living that
          is an old man and no honester than I.

DOGBERRY Comparisons are odorous: *palabras*, neighbour Verges.[114]

LEONATO   Neighbours, you are tedious.

DOGBERRY It pleases your Worship to say so, but we are the poor
          Duke's officers. But truly, for mine own part, if I were
          as tedious as a king, I could find in my heart to bestow
          it all of your Worship.[115]

LEONATO   All thy tediousness on me, ah?   20

DOGBERRY Yea, an 'twere a thousand pound more than 'tis, for I
          hear as good exclamation on your Worship as of any
          man in the city, and though I be but a poor man, I am
          glad to hear it.

VERGES   And so am I.

LEONATO   I would fain know what you have to say.

VERGES   Marry sir, our watch tonight, excepting your Worship's
          presence,[116] ha' ta'en a couple of as arrant knaves as any
          in Messina.

DOGBERRY A good old man, sir, he will be talking; as they say,   30
          'When the age is in, the wit is out.' God help us, it is
          a world to see. — Well said, i'faith, neighbour Verges.
          — Well, God's a good man; an two men ride of a
          horse, one must ride behind. An honest soul, i'faith,
          sir, by my troth he is, as ever broke bread, but — God is
          to be worshipped — all men are not alike, alas, good
          neighbour.

LEONATO   Indeed, neighbour, he comes too short of you.

DOGBERRY Gifts that God gives.

LEONATO   I must leave you.   40

DOGBERRY One word, sir: our watch, sir, have indeed compre-
          hended two aspitious persons,[117] and we would have
          them this morning examined before your Worship.

LEONATO   Take their examination yourself, and bring it me. I am now in great haste, as it may appear unto you.

DOGBERRY It shall be suffigance.

LEONATO Drink some wine ere you go. Fare you well.

Enter a MESSENGER.

MESSEN. My lord, they stay for you to give your daughter to her husband.

LEONATO I'll wait upon them; I am ready.   50

[*Exeunt Leonato and the messenger.*

DOGBERRY Go, good partner, go get you to Francis Seacoal;[118] bid him bring his pen and inkhorn to the gaol: we are now to examination these men.

VERGES And we must do it wisely.

DOGBERRY We will spare for no wit, I warrant you: here's that shall drive some of them to a non-come. Only get the learnèd writer to set down our excommunication, and meet me at the gaol.[119]

[*Exeunt.*

ACT 4, SCENE I.

Before the altar of a church.

Enter DON PEDRO, DON JOHN, LEONATO, FRIAR FRANCIS,
CLAUDIO, BENEDICK, HERO *and* BEATRICE.

LEONATO   Come, Friar Francis, be brief: only to the plain form of
           marriage, and you shall recount their particular duties
           afterwards.

FRIAR   [*turning to Claudio:*] You come hither, my lord, to marry
           this lady?

CLAUDIO   No.

LEONATO   To be married to her. Friar, you come to marry her.

FRIAR   [*to Hero:*] Lady, you come hither to be married to this
           Count?

HERO   I do.   10

FRIAR   If either of you know any inward impediment why
           you should not be conjoined, I charge you on your
           souls to utter it.[120]

CLAUDIO   Know you any, Hero?

HERO   None, my lord.

FRIAR   Know you any, Count?

LEONATO   I dare make his answer, 'None'.

CLAUDIO   O, what men dare do! What men may do! What men
           daily do, not knowing what they do!

BENEDICK   How now? Interjections? Why then, some be of laughing,   20
           as 'Ah! ha! he!'[121]

CLAUDIO   Stand thee by, Friar. – Father, by your leave:
           Will you with free and unconstrainèd soul
           Give me this maid, your daughter?

LEONATO   As freely, son, as God did give her me.

CLAUDIO   And what have I to give you back whose worth
           May counterpoise this rich and precious gift?

D. PEDRO   Nothing, unless you render her again.

CLAUDIO   Sweet Prince, you learn me noble thankfulness.
           – There, Leonato, take her back again.   30
           Give not this rotten orange to your friend;

She's but the sign and semblance of her honour.
Behold how like a maid she blushes here!
O, what authority and show of truth
Can cunning sin cover itself withal!
Comes not that blood as modest evidence
To witness simple virtue? Would you not swear,
All you that see her, that she were a maid,
By these exterior shows? But she is none:
She knows the heat of a luxurious bed;   40
Her blush is guiltiness, not modesty.

LEONATO   What do you mean, my lord?

CLAUDIO   Not to be married:
Not to knit my soul to an approvèd wanton.

LEONATO   Dear my lord, if you in your own proof
Have vanquished the resistance of her youth,
And made defeat of her virginity —

CLAUDIO   I know what you would say: if I have known her,
You will say she did embrace me as a husband,
And so extenuate the 'forehand sin.
No, Leonato,   50
I never tempted her with word too large,
But, as a brother to his sister, showed
Bashful sincerity and comely love.

HERO   And seemed I ever otherwise to you?

CLAUDIO   Out on thee, seeming![122] I will write against it.
You seem to me as Dian in her orb,
As chaste as is the bud ere it be blown;
But you are more intemperate in your blood
Than Venus or those pampered animals
That rage in savage sensuality.   60

HERO   Is my lord well, that he doth speak so wide?

LEONATO   Sweet Prince, why speak not you?

D. PEDRO   What should I speak?
I stand dishonoured that have gone about
To link my dear friend to a common stale.

LEONATO   Are these things spoken, or do I but dream?

DON JOHN   Sir, they are spoken, and these things are true.

BENEDICK   This looks not like a nuptial.

HERO   'True'? O God!

CLAUDIO   Leonato, stand I here?
Is this the Prince? Is this the Prince's brother?
Is this face Hero's? Are our eyes our own?   70

LEONATO   All this is so, but what of this, my lord?

CLAUDIO   Let me but move one question to your daughter,
And by that fatherly and kindly power
That you have in her, bid her answer truly.

LEONATO   [to Hero:] I charge thee do so, as thou art my child.

HERO   O God defend me! How am I beset!
What kind of catechizing call you this?

CLAUDIO   To make you answer truly to your name.

HERO   Is it not Hero? Who can blot that name
With any just reproach?

CLAUDIO   Marry, that can Hero: 80
Hero itself can blot out Hero's virtue.
What man was he talked with you yesternight,
Out at your window betwixt twelve and one?
Now if you are a maid, answer to this.

HERO   I talked with no man at that hour, my lord.

D. PEDRO   Why, then are you no maiden. – Leonato,
I am sorry you must hear: upon mine honour,
Myself, my brother and this grievèd Count
Did see her, hear her, at that hour last night,
Talk with a ruffian at her chamber-window,   90
Who hath indeed, most like a liberal villain,
Confessed the vile encounters they have had
A thousand times in secret.

DON JOHN   Fie, fie! They are not to be named, my lord,
Not to be spoke of.
There is not chastity enough in language,
Without offence to utter them. – Thus, pretty lady,
I am sorry for thy much misgovernment.

CLAUDIO   O Hero! What a Hero hadst thou been,
If half thy outward graces had been placed   100
About the thoughts and counsels of thy heart!
But, fare thee well, most foul, most fair; farewell,
Thou pure impiety and impious purity.
For thee I'll lock up all the gates of love,
And on my eyelids shall conjecture hang,

	To turn all beauty into thoughts of harm,
	And never shall it more be gracious.
LEONATO	Hath no man's dagger here a point for me?

[Hero faints.

BEATRICE	Why, how now cousin, wherefore sink you down?
DON JOHN	Come let us go. These things, come thus to light, 110
	Smother her spirits up.

[Exeunt Don Pedro, Don John and Claudio.

BENEDICK	How doth the lady?
BEATRICE	Dead, I think. — Help, uncle —
	Hero! Why, Hero! — Uncle — Signior Benedick — Friar!
LEONATO	O Fate! Take not away thy heavy hand.
	Death is the fairest cover for her shame
	That may be wished for.
BEATRICE	How now, cousin Hero?
FRIAR	[*to Hero:*] Have comfort, lady.
LEONATO	[*to Hero:*] Dost thou look up?
FRIAR	Yea, wherefore should she not?
LEONATO	Wherefore? Why, doth not every earthly thing
	Cry shame upon her? Could she here deny 120
	The story that is printed in her blood?
	— Do not live, Hero, do not ope thine eyes:
	For, did I think thou wouldst not quickly die,
	Thought I thy spirits were stronger than thy shames,
	Myself would on the rearward of reproaches
	Strike at thy life. Grieved I, I had but one?
	Chid I for that at frugal Nature's frame?
	O, one too much by thee. Why had I one?
	Why ever wast thou lovely in my eyes?
	Why had I not with charitable hand 130
	Took up a beggar's issue at my gates,
	Who, smirchèd thus, and mired with infamy,
	I might have said, 'No part of it is mine:
	This shame derives itself from unknown loins'?
	But mine, and mine I loved, and mine I praised,
	And mine that I was proud on, mine so much
	That I myself was to myself not mine,
	Valuing of her — why she, O she is fall'n
	Into a pit of ink, that the wide sea

	Hath drops too few to wash her clean again, 140
	And salt too little which may season give
	To her foul tainted flesh.
BENEDICK	Sir, sir, be patient. For my part, I am so
	Attired in wonder, I know not what to say.[123]
BEATRICE	O, on my soul, my cousin is belied!
BENEDICK	Lady, were you her bedfellow last night?
BEATRICE	No, truly, not; although, until last night,
	I have this twelvemonth been her bedfellow.
LEONATO	Confirmed, confirmed! O, that is stronger made,
	Which was before barred up with ribs of iron. 150
	Would the two princes lie, and Claudio lie,
	Who loved her so, that, speaking of her foulness,
	Washed it with tears? Hence from her, let her die.
FRIAR	Hear me a little;
	For I have only been silent so long,
	And given way unto this course of fortune,
	By noting of the lady. I have marked
	A thousand blushing apparitions[124]
	To start into her face, a thousand innocent shames
	In angel whiteness beat away those blushes, 160
	And in her eye there hath appeared a fire
	To burn the errors that these princes hold
	Against her maiden truth. Call me a fool,
	Trust not my reading, nor my observations,
	Which with experimental seal doth warrant
	The tenure of my book;[125] trust not my age,
	My reverence, calling, nor divinity,
	If this sweet lady lie not guiltless here
	Under some biting error. [*Hero slowly recovers.*
LEONATO	Friar, it cannot be.
	Thou seest that all the grace that she hath left 170
	Is that she will not add to her damnation
	A sin of perjury: she not denies it.
	Why seek'st thou then to cover with excuse
	That which appears in proper nakedness?
FRIAR	Lady, what man is he you are accused of?
HERO	They know that do accuse me, I know none.
	If I know more of any man alive

Than that which maiden modesty doth warrant,
Let all my sins lack mercy. — O my father,
Prove you that any man with me conversed   180
At hours unmeet, or that I yesternight
Maintained the change of words with any creature,
Refuse me, hate me, torture me to death!

FRIAR   There is some strange misprision in the princes.

BENEDICK Two of them have the very bent of honour;
And if their wisdoms be misled in this,
The practice of it lives in John the bastard,
Whose spirits toil in frame of villainies.

LEONATO I know not. If they speak but truth of her,
These hands shall tear her; if they wrong her honour,   190
The proudest of them shall well hear of it.
Time hath not yet so dried this blood of mine,
Nor age so eat up my invention,
Nor Fortune made such havoc of my means,
Nor my bad life reft me so much of friends,
But they shall find, awaked in such a kind,
Both strength of limb, and policy of mind,
Ability in means, and choice of friends,
To quit me of them throughly.

FRIAR   Pause awhile,
And let my counsel sway you in this case.   200
Your daughter here the princes left for dead.
Let her awhile be secretly kept in,
And publish it that she is dead indeed.
Maintain a mourning ostentation,
And on your family's old monument
Hang mournful epitaphs, and do all rites
That appertain unto a burial.

LEONATO What shall become of this? What will this do?

FRIAR   Marry, this, well carried, shall on her behalf
Change slander to remorse: that is some good.   210
But not for that dream I on this strange course,
But on this travail look for greater birth:
She, dying (as it must be so maintained)
Upon the instant that she was accused,
Shall be lamented, pitied, and excused

Of every hearer: for it so falls out
That what we have, we prize not to the worth
Whiles we enjoy it; but being lacked and lost,
Why then we rack the value, then we find
The virtue that possession would not show us   220
Whiles it was ours. So will it fare with Claudio.
When he shall hear she died upon his words,
Th'idea of her life shall sweetly creep
Into his study of imagination,
And every lovely organ of her life
Shall come apparelled in more precious habit,
More moving-delicate and full of life,
Into the eye and prospect of his soul
Than when she lived indeed: then shall he mourn,
If ever love had interest in his liver,[126]   230
And wish he had not so accusèd her –
No, though he thought his accusation true.
Let this be so, and doubt not but success
Will fashion the event in better shape
Than I can lay it down in likelihood.
But if all aim but this be levelled false,
The supposition of the lady's death
Will quench the wonder of her infamy.[127]
And if it sort not well, you may conceal her,
As best befits her wounded reputation,   240
In some reclusive and religious life,
Out of all eyes, tongues, minds and injuries.

BENEDICK Signior Leonato, let the Friar advise you;
And though you know my inwardness and love
Is very much unto the Prince and Claudio,
Yet, by mine honour, I will deal in this
As secretly and justly as your soul
Should with your body.

LEONATO   Being that I flow in grief,
The smallest twine may lead me.

FRIAR 'Tis well consented – presently away –   250
     For to strange sores strangely they strain the cure.[128]
Come lady, die to live: this wedding day
     Perhaps is but prolonged: have patience and endure.

[Exeunt Friar, Hero and Leonato.

BENEDICK Lady Beatrice, have you wept all this while?

BEATRICE Yea, and I will weep a while longer.

BENEDICK I will not desire that.

BEATRICE You have no reason; I do it freely.

BENEDICK Surely I do believe your fair cousin is wronged.

BEATRICE Ah, how much might the man deserve of me that
would right her!   260

BENEDICK Is there any way to show such friendship?

BEATRICE A very even way, but no such friend.

BENEDICK May a man do it?

BEATRICE It is a man's office, but not yours.

BENEDICK I do love nothing in the world so well as you: is not
that strange?

BEATRICE As strange as the thing I know not. It were as possible
for me to say I loved nothing so well as you, but
believe me not; and yet I lie not; I confess nothing,
nor I deny nothing. I am sorry for my cousin.   270

BENEDICK By my sword, Beatrice, thou lovest me.

BEATRICE Do not swear and eat it.

BENEDICK I will swear by it that you love me, and I will make him
eat it that says I love not you.

BEATRICE Will you not eat your word?

BENEDICK With no sauce that can be devised to it. I protest I love
thee.

BEATRICE Why then, God forgive me —

BENEDICK What offence, sweet Beatrice?

BEATRICE You have stayed me in a happy hour: I was about to   280
protest I loved you.

BENEDICK And do it with all thy heart.

BEATRICE I love you with so much of my heart, that none is left
to protest.

BENEDICK Come, bid me do anything for thee.

BEATRICE Kill Claudio!

BENEDICK Ha! Not for the wide world.

BEATRICE You kill me to deny it. Farewell.

BENEDICK Tarry, sweet Beatrice.   *[He detains her.*

BEATRICE I am gone, though I am here; there is no love in you;   290
nay, I pray you let me go.

BENEDICK Beatrice –

BEATRICE In faith, I will go.

BENEDICK We'll be friends first.

BEATRICE You dare easier be friends with me than fight with mine enemy.

BENEDICK Is Claudio thine enemy?

BEATRICE Is a not approved in the height a villain, that hath slandered, scorned, dishonoured my kinswoman? O that I were a man! What, bear her in hand until they 300 come to take hands, and then, with public accusation, uncovered slander, unmitigated rancour – O God, that I were a man! I would eat his heart in the market-place.

BENEDICK Hear me, Beatrice –

BEATRICE Talk with a man out at a window – a proper saying!

BENEDICK Nay, but Beatrice –

BEATRICE Sweet Hero, she is wronged, she is slandered, she is undone.

BENEDICK Beat–

BEATRICE Princes and counties! Surely a princely testimony, a 310 goodly count, Count Comfect – a sweet gallant, surely. O that I were a man for his sake! Or that I had any friend would be a man for my sake! But manhood is melted into curtsies, valour into compliment, and men are only turned into tongue, and trim ones too: he is now as valiant as Hercules, that only tells a lie and swears it. I cannot be a man with wishing, therefore I will die a woman with grieving.

BENEDICK Tarry, good Beatrice; by this hand, I love thee.

BEATRICE Use it for my love some other way than swearing by it. 320

BENEDICK Think you in your soul the Count Claudio hath wronged Hero?

BEATRICE Yea, as sure as I have a thought or a soul.

BENEDICK Enough; I am engaged: I will challenge him. I will kiss your hand, and so I leave you. [*He kisses her hand.*] By this hand, Claudio shall render me a dear account. As you hear of me, so think of me. Go comfort your cousin; I must say she is dead; and so farewell.

[*Exit Benedick; Beatrice follows.*

SCENE 2.

A room in a prison.

Enter DOGBERRY, VERGES[129] *and the* SEXTON *(all in gowns),*
with the WATCHMEN *guarding* CONRADE *and* BORACHIO.

DOGBERRY Is our whole dissembly appeared?
VERGES O, a stool and a cushion for the sexton.
                    [*These are brought.*
SEXTON [*sits.*] Which be the malefactors?
DOGBERRY Marry, that am I, and my partner.
VERGES Nay, that's certain: we have the exhibition to examine.
SEXTON But which are the offenders that are to be examined?
          Let them come before Master Constable.
DOGBERRY Yea, marry, let them come before me.
                    [*Borachio and Conrade are led forward.*
          What is your name, friend?
BORACHIO Borachio.   10
DOGBERRY [*to the sexton:*] Pray write down 'Borachio'. [*To Conrade:*]
          Yours, sirrah?
CONRADE I am a gentleman, sir, and my name is Conrade.
DOGBERRY Write down 'Master Gentleman Conrade'. – Masters,
          do you serve God?
CONRADE, BORACHIO Yea, sir, we hope.
DOGBERRY Write down that they hope they serve God; and write
          'God' first, for God defend but God should go before
          such villains. – Masters, it is proved already that you
          are little better than false knaves, and it will go near to 20
          be thought so shortly. How answer you for yourselves?
CONRADE Marry, sir, we say we are none.
DOGBERRY [*to Verges:*] A marvellous witty fellow, I assure you; but
          I will go about with him. [*To Borachio:*] Come you
          hither, sirrah: a word in your ear. Sir, I say to you, it is
          thought you are false knaves.
BORACHIO Sir, I say to you, we are none.
DOGBERRY Well, stand aside. – 'Fore God, they are both in a tale.
          Have you writ down, that they are none?

SEXTON   Master Constable, you go not the way to examine. 30
You must call forth the watch that are their accusers.

DOGBERRY Yea, marry, that's the eftest way: let the watch come
forth. [*To the watchmen:*] Masters, I charge you in the
Prince's name, accuse these men.

WATCH. I This man said, sir, that Don John, the Prince's brother,
was a villain.

DOGBERRY Write down 'Prince John a villain'. Why this is flat
perjury, to call a prince's brother villain.

BORACHIO Master Constable –

DOGBERRY Pray thee, fellow, peace. I do not like thy look, I 40
promise thee.

SEXTON   What heard you him say else?

WATCH. 2 Marry, that he had received a thousand ducats of Don
John, for accusing the Lady Hero wrongfully.

DOGBERRY Flat burglary as ever was committed.

VERGES   Yea, by Mass; that it is.

SEXTON   What else, fellow?

WATCH. I And that Count Claudio did mean, upon his words, to
disgrace Hero before the whole assembly, and not
marry her.   50

DOGBERRY [*to Borachio:*] O villain! Thou wilt be condemned into
everlasting redemption for this.

SEXTON   What else?

WATCHMEN This is all.

SEXTON   [*to Borachio and Conrade:*] And this is more, masters, than
you can deny. Prince John is this morning secretly
stolen away; Hero was in this manner accused, in this
very manner refused, and upon the grief of this suddenly
died. – Master Constable, let these men be bound, and
brought to Leonato's. I will go before and show him 60
their examination.   [*Exit.*

DOGBERRY Come, let them be opinioned.

CONRADE Let them be in the hands of coxcomb.[130]

DOGBERRY God's my life, where's the sexton? Let him write down
'the Prince's officer "coxcomb" '. Come, bind them. –
Thou naughty varlet!

CONRADE Away! You are an ass, you are an ass.
                              [*The watchmen bind Borachio and Conrade.*

DOGBERRY Dost thou not suspect my place? Dost thou not suspect
my years? – O, that he were here to write me down an
ass! But, masters, remember that I am an ass; though it   70
be not written down, yet forget not that I am an ass. –
No, thou villain, thou art full of piety, as shall be
proved upon thee by good witness. I am a wise fellow,
and, which is more, an officer, and, which is more, a
householder, and, which is more, as pretty a piece of
flesh as any is in Messina, and one that knows the law,
go to, and a rich fellow enough, go to, and a fellow
that hath had losses, and one that hath two gowns and
everything handsome about him. – Bring him away.
O, that I had been writ down an ass!   80

[*Exeunt.*

ACT 5, SCENE 1.

In front of Leonato's house.

Enter LEONATO *and* ANTONIO.

ANTONIO If you go on thus, you will kill yourself,
And 'tis not wisdom thus to second grief
Against yourself.

LEONATO   I pray thee cease thy counsel,
Which falls into mine ears as profitless
As water in a sieve. Give not me counsel,
Nor let no comforter delight mine ear
But such a one whose wrongs do suit with mine.
Bring me a father that so loved his child,
Whose joy of her is overwhelmed like mine,
And bid him speak of patience;   10
Measure his woe the length and breadth of mine,
And let it answer every strain for strain,
As thus for thus, and such a grief for such,
In every lineament, branch, shape, and form.
If such a one will smile and stroke his beard,
And sorrow; wag, cry 'hem' when he should groan;[131]
Patch grief with proverbs, make misfortune drunk
With candle-wasters: bring him yet to me,
And I of him will gather patience.[132]
But there is no such man, for, brother, men   20
Can counsel and speak comfort to that grief
Which they themselves not feel, but, tasting it,
Their counsel turns to passion, which before
Would give preceptial medicine to rage,
Fetter strong madness in a silken thread,
Charm ache with air, and agony with words.
No, no; 'tis all men's office to speak patience
To those that wring under the load of sorrow,
But no man's virtue nor sufficiency
To be so moral when he shall endure   30
The like himself: therefore give me no counsel.
My griefs cry louder than advertisement.

ANTONIO   Therein do men from children nothing differ.

LEONATO   I pray thee peace; I will be flesh and blood,
For there was never yet philosopher
That could endure the toothache patiently,
However they have writ the style of gods,
And made a push at chance and sufferance.[133]

ANTONIO   Yet bend not all the harm upon yourself:
Make those that do offend you suffer too.   40

LEONATO   There thou speak'st reason; nay, I will do so.
My soul doth tell me Hero is belied,
And that shall Claudio know, so shall the Prince,
And all of them that thus dishonour her.

        Enter DON PEDRO *and* CLAUDIO.

ANTONIO   Here comes the Prince and Claudio hastily.

D. PEDRO   Good-den, good-den.

CLAUDIO   Good day to both of you.
                         [*They pass by.*

LEONATO   Hear you, my lords?

D. PEDRO   We have some haste, Leonato.

LEONATO   'Some haste', my lord! Well, fare you well, my lord.
Are you so hasty now? Well, all is one.

D. PEDRO   Nay, do not quarrel with us, good old man.   50

ANTONIO   If he could right himself with quarrelling,
Some of us would lie low.

CLAUDIO   Who wrongs him?

LEONATO   Marry, *thou* dost wrong me, thou dissembler, thou.
Nay, never lay thy hand upon thy sword:
I fear thee not.

CLAUDIO   Marry, beshrew my hand,
If it should give your age such cause of fear.
In faith, my hand meant nothing to my sword.

LEONATO   Tush, tush, man, never fleer and jest at me.
I speak not like a dotard nor a fool,
As under privilege of age to brag   60
What I have done being young, or what would do
Were I not old. Know, Claudio, to thy head,
Thou hast so wronged mine innocent child and me
That I am forced to lay my reverence by,
And with grey hairs and bruise of many days

Do challenge thee to trial of a man.
I say thou hast belied mine innocent child,
Thy slander hath gone through and through her heart,
And she lies buried with her ancestors:
O, in a tomb where never scandal slept,   70
Save this of hers, framed by thy villainy.

CLAUDIO My villainy?

LEONATO   Thine, Claudio; thine, I say.

D. PEDRO You say not right, old man.

LEONATO [*indicating his sword:*]   My lord, my lord,
I'll prove it on his body if he dare,
Despite his nice fence and his active practice,
His May of youth and bloom of lustihood.

CLAUDIO Away, I will not have to do with you.

LEONATO Canst thou so daff me? Thou hast killed my child;
If thou kill'st me, boy, thou shalt kill a man.

ANTONIO He shall kill two of us, and men indeed;   80
But that's no matter, let him kill one first.

                              [*He draws his sword.*
Win me and wear me! Let him answer me.[134] –
Come follow me boy, come sir boy, come follow me,
Sir boy, I'll whip you from your foining fence:
Nay, as I am a gentleman, I will.

LEONATO Brother –

ANTONIO Content yourself. God knows I loved my niece,
And she is dead, slandered to death by villains
That dare as well answer a man indeed
As I dare take a serpent by the tongue.   90
Boys, apes, braggarts, Jacks, milksops!

LEONATO   Brother Antony –

ANTONIO Hold you content. What, man! I know them, yea,
And what they weigh, even to the utmost scruple:
Scambling, out-facing, fashion-monging boys,
That lie, and cog, and flout, deprave, and slander,
Go anticly, and show outward hideousness,
And speak off half a dozen dangerous words,
How they might hurt their enemies, if they durst;
And this is all.

LEONATO But brother Antony –

ANTONIO	Come, 'tis no matter; 100
	Do not you meddle, let me deal in this.
D. PEDRO	Gentlemen both, we will not wake your patience.
	My heart is sorry for your daughter's death;
	But, on my honour, she was charged with nothing
	But what was true and very full of proof.
LEONATO	My lord, my lord —
D. PEDRO	I will not hear you.
LEONATO	No? — Come brother, away. — I will be heard.
ANTONIO	And shall, or some of us will smart for it.[135]

                              [*Exeunt Leonato and Antonio.*

                         Enter BENEDICK.

D. PEDRO   See, see, here comes the man we went to seek.

CLAUDIO   Now, signior, what news?   110

BENEDICK   Good day, my lord.

D. PEDRO   Welcome, signior; you are almost come to part almost
            a fray.

CLAUDIO   We had liked to have had our two noses snapped off
            with two old men without teeth.[136]

D. PEDRO   Leonato and his brother. What think'st thou? Had we
            fought, I doubt we should have been too young for
            them.

BENEDICK   In a false quarrel there is no true valour. I came to seek
            you both.   120

CLAUDIO   We have been up and down to seek thee, for we are
            high-proof melancholy, and would fain have it beaten
            away. Wilt thou use thy wit?

BENEDICK   It is in my scabbard; shall I draw it?

D. PEDRO   Dost thou wear thy wit by thy side?

CLAUDIO   Never any did so, though very many have been beside
            their wit. I will bid thee draw, as we do the minstrels:
            draw to pleasure us.[137]

D. PEDRO   As I am an honest man, he looks pale. — Art thou sick,
            or angry?   130

CLAUDIO   What, courage, man! What though care killed a cat?
            Thou hast mettle enough in thee to kill care.

BENEDICK   Sir, I shall meet your wit in the career, and you charge
            it against me. I pray you choose another subject.

CLAUDIO   [*to Don Pedro:*] Nay then, give him another staff; this
            last was broke cross.
D. PEDRO   By this light, he changes more and more. I think he be
            angry indeed.
CLAUDIO   If he be, he knows how to turn his girdle.
BENEDICK   [*to Claudio:*] Shall I speak a word in your ear?   140
CLAUDIO   God bless me from a challenge!
BENEDICK   [*quietly:*] You are a villain. I jest not. I will make it
            good how you dare, with what you dare, and when
            you dare. Do me right, or I will protest your coward-
            ice. You have killed a sweet lady, and her death shall
            fall heavy on you. [*Loudly:*] Let me hear from you.
CLAUDIO   Well, I will meet you, so I may have good cheer.¹³⁸
D. PEDRO   What, a feast, a feast?
CLAUDIO   I'faith, I thank him, he hath bid me to a calf's-head and
            a capon, the which if I do not carve most curiously, say   150
            my knife's naught. Shall I not find a woodcock too?¹³⁹
BENEDICK   Sir, your wit ambles well; it goes easily.
D. PEDRO   I'll tell thee how Beatrice praised thy wit the other day.
            I said, thou hadst a fine wit. 'True,' said she, 'a fine
            little one'; 'No,' said I, 'a great wit'; 'Right,' says she, 'a
            great gross one'; 'Nay,' said I, 'a good wit'; 'Just,' said
            she, 'it hurts nobody'; 'Nay,' said I, 'the gentleman is
            wise'; 'Certain,' said she, 'a wise gentleman';¹⁴⁰ 'Nay,'
            said I, 'he hath the tongues'; 'That I believe,' said she,
            'for he swore a thing to me on Monday night, which   160
            he forswore on Tuesday morning: there's a double
            tongue, there's two tongues.' Thus did she an hour
            together trans-shape thy particular virtues; yet at last
            she concluded, with a sigh, thou wast the proper'st
            man in Italy.
CLAUDIO   For the which she wept heartily and said she cared not.
D. PEDRO   Yea, that she did; but yet, for all that, and if she did
            not hate him deadly, she would love him dearly. The
            old man's daughter told us all.
CLAUDIO   All, all; and moreover, God saw him when he was hid   170
            in the garden.¹⁴¹
D. PEDRO   But when shall we set the savage bull's horns on the
            sensible Benedick's head?

CLAUDIO   Yea, and text underneath, 'Here dwells Benedick the married man'?[142]

BENEDICK Fare you well, boy; you know my mind. I will leave you now to your gossip-like humour. You break jests as braggarts do their blades, which, God be thanked, hurt not.[143] – My lord, for your many courtesies I thank you. I must discontinue your company. Your 180 brother the bastard is fled from Messina. You have among you killed a sweet and innocent lady. For my Lord Lack-beard, there, he and I shall meet; and till then, peace be with him.   [Exit.

D. PEDRO He is in earnest.

CLAUDIO   In most profound earnest, and, I'll warrant you, for the love of Beatrice.

D. PEDRO And hath challenged thee?

CLAUDIO   Most sincerely.

D. PEDRO What a pretty thing man is, when he goes in his 190 doublet and hose and leaves off his wit!

CLAUDIO   He is then a giant to an ape, but then is an ape a doctor to such a man.

D. PEDRO But soft you, let me be. Pluck up, my heart, and be sad.[144] did he not say my brother was fled?

Enter DOGBERRY, VERGES *and the* WATCHMEN *escorting*
CONRADE *and* BORACHIO.[145]

DOGBERRY [*to Conrade:*] Come you sir, if justice cannot tame you, she shall ne'er weigh more reasons in her balance. Nay, and you be a cursing hypocrite once, you must be looked to.

D. PEDRO How now, two of my brother's men bound? Borachio one.   200

CLAUDIO   Hearken after their offence, my lord.

D. PEDRO Officers, what offence have these men done?

DOGBERRY Marry sir, they have committed false report; moreover, they have spoken untruths; secondarily, they are slanders; sixth and lastly, they have belied a lady; thirdly, they have verified unjust things; and to conclude, they are lying knaves.

D. PEDRO First, I ask thee what they have done; thirdly, I ask thee what's their offence; sixth and lastly, why they are

committed; and to conclude, what you lay to their 210
charge.

CLAUDIO   Rightly reasoned, and in his own division; and, by my
troth, there's one meaning well suited.[146]

D. PEDRO   Who have you offended, masters, that you are thus
bound to your answer? This learnèd constable is too
cunning to be understood. What's your offence?

BORACHIO Sweet Prince, let me go no farther to mine answer: do
you hear me, and let this Count kill me. I have deceived
even your very eyes. What your wisdoms could not
discover, these shallow fools have brought to light, who 220
in the night overheard me confessing to this man how
Don John, your brother, incensed me to slander the
Lady Hero, how you were brought into the orchard
and saw me court Margaret in Hero's garments, how
you disgraced her when you should marry her. My
villainy they have upon record, which I had rather seal
with my death than repeat over to my shame. The lady
is dead upon mine and my master's false accusation;
and, briefly, I desire nothing but the reward of a villain.

D. PEDRO   [to Claudio:] Runs not this speech like iron through 230
your blood?

CLAUDIO   I have drunk poison whiles he uttered it.

D. PEDRO   [to Borochio:] But did my brother set thee on to this?

BORACHIO Yea, and paid me richly for the practice of it.

D. PEDRO   He is composed and framed of treachery,
And fled he is upon this villainy.

CLAUDIO   Sweet Hero, now thy image doth appear
In the rare semblance that I loved it first.

DOGBERRY [to watchmen:] Come, bring away the plaintiffs: by this
time our sexton hath reformed Signior Leonato of the 240
matter; and masters, do not forget to specify, when time
and place shall serve, that I am an ass.

VERGES   Here, here comes Master Signior Leonato, and the
sexton too.

        Enter LEONATO, ANTONIO and the SEXTON.

LEONATO   Which is the villain? Let me see his eyes,
That when I note another man like him,

I may avoid him. Which of these is he?

BORACHIO If you would know your wronger, look on me.

LEONATO   Art thou the slave that with thy breath hast killed
Mine innocent child?

BORACHIO   Yea, even I alone.   250

LEONATO   No, not so, villain: thou beliest thyself.
Here stand a pair of honourable men
(A third is fled) that had a hand in it.
I thank you, princes, for my daughter's death.
Record it with your high and worthy deeds:
'Twas bravely done, if you bethink you of it.

CLAUDIO   I know not how to pray your patience,
Yet I must speak. Choose your revenge yourself,
Impose me to what penance your invention
Can lay upon my sin; yet sinned I not,   260
But in mistaking.

D. PEDRO   By my soul, nor I;
And yet, to satisfy this good old man,
I would bend under any heavy weight
That he'll enjoin me to.

LEONATO   I cannot bid you bid my daughter live –
That were impossible – but I pray you both,
Possess the people in Messina here
How innocent she died; and if your love
Can labour aught in sad invention,[147]
Hang her an epitaph upon her tomb,   270
And sing it to her bones, sing it tonight.
Tomorrow morning come you to my house,
And since you could not be my son-in-law,
Be yet my nephew. My brother hath a daughter,
Almost the copy of my child that's dead,
And she alone is heir to both of us.[148]
Give her the right you should have giv'n her cousin,
And so dies my revenge.

CLAUDIO   O noble sir!
Your over-kindness doth wring tears from me.
I do embrace your offer, and dispose   280
For henceforth of poor Claudio.

LEONATO   Tomorrow then I will expect your coming;

Tonight I take my leave. This naughty man
Shall face to face be brought to Margaret,
Who I believe was packed in all this wrong,
Hired to it by your brother.
BORACHIO   No, by my soul, she was not,
Nor knew not what she did when she spoke to me,
But always hath been just and virtuous
In anything that I do know by her.
DOGBERRY Moreover, sir, which indeed is not under white and 290
black, this plaintiff here, the offender, did call me 'ass':
I beseech you, let it be remembered in his punishment;
and also the watch heard them talk of one Deformed:
they say he wears a key in his ear and a lock hanging by
it, and borrows money in God's name, the which he
hath used so long, and never paid, that now men grow
hard-hearted and will lend nothing for God's sake. Pray
you examine him upon that point.
LEONATO I thank thee for thy care and honest pains.
DOGBERRY Your Worship speaks like a most thankful and reverend 300
youth, and I praise God for you.
LEONATO [giving him money:] There's for thy pains.
DOGBERRY God save the foundation!149
LEONATO Go, I discharge thee of thy prisoner, and I thank thee.
DOGBERRY I leave an arrant knave with your Worship, which I
beseech your Worship to correct yourself, for the ex-
ample of others. God keep your Worship, I wish your
Worship well, God restore you to health, I humbly
give you leave to depart, and, if a merry meeting may
be wished, God prohibit it. Come, neighbour.   310
                              [Exeunt Dogberry and Verges.
LEONATO Until tomorrow morning, lords, farewell.
ANTONIO Farewell, my lords; we look for you tomorrow.
D. PEDRO We will not fail.
CLAUDIO   Tonight I'll mourn with Hero.
                    [Exeunt Don Pedro and Claudio.
LEONATO [to the watchmen:]
Bring you these fellows on. We'll talk with Margaret,
How her acquaintance grew with this lewd fellow.
                              [Exeunt.

SCENE 2.

Near Leonato's house.

Enter BENEDICK *and* MARGARET.

BENEDICK Pray thee, sweet Mistress Margaret, deserve well at my
hands by helping me to the speech of Beatrice.

MARGARET Will you then write me a sonnet in praise of my beauty?

BENEDICK In so high a style, Margaret, that no man living shall
come over it, for in most comely truth thou deservest it.

MARGARET To have no man come over me? Why, shall I always
keep below stairs?[150]

BENEDICK Thy wit is as quick as the greyhound's mouth: it
catches.

MARGARET And yours as blunt as the fencer's foils, which hit but   10
hurt not.

BENEDICK A most manly wit, Margaret: it will not hurt a woman;
and so I pray thee call Beatrice. I give thee the bucklers.

MARGARET Give us the swords; we have bucklers of our own.

BENEDICK If you use them, Margaret, you must put in the pikes
with a vice — and they are dangerous weapons for maids.

MARGARET Well, I will call Beatrice to you, who I think hath legs.

BENEDICK And therefore will come.[151]   [*Exit Margaret.*

[*He sings:*]   The god of love,
                  That sits above,   20
            And knows me, and knows me,
               How pitiful I deserve[152] —

I mean in singing; but in loving, Leander the good
swimmer, Troilus the first employer of pandars, and a
whole bookful of these quondam carpet-mongers
whose names yet run smoothly in the even road of a
blank verse, why, they were never so truly turned over
and over as my poor self in love. Marry, I cannot show
it in rhyme; I have tried. I can find out no rhyme to
'lady' but 'baby', an innocent rhyme; for 'scorn', 'horn,' 30
a hard rhyme: for 'school', 'fool', a babbling rhyme:
very ominous endings. No, I was not born under a
rhyming planet, nor I cannot woo in festival terms. [153]

Enter BEATRICE.

Sweet Beatrice, wouldst thou come when I called thee?

BEATRICE   Yea, signior, and depart when you bid me.

BENEDICK   O, stay but till then.

BEATRICE   'Then' is spoken: fare you well now; and yet, ere I go,
let me go with that I came for, which is, with knowing
what hath passed between you and Claudio.

BENEDICK   Only foul words; and thereupon I will kiss thee.   40

BEATRICE   Foul words is but foul wind, and foul wind is but foul
breath, and foul breath is noisome; therefore I will
depart unkissed.

BENEDICK   Thou hast frighted the word out of his right sense, so
forcible is thy wit; but I must tell thee plainly, Claudio
undergoes my challenge, and either I must shortly hear
from him, or I will subscribe him a coward; and I pray
thee now tell me, for which of my bad parts didst thou
first fall in love with me?

BEATRICE   For them all together, which maintain so politic a state   50
of evil that they will not admit any good part to
intermingle with them; but for which of my good
parts did you first suffer love for me?

BENEDICK   'Suffer love'! A good epithet. I do suffer love indeed,
for I love thee against my will.

BEATRICE   In spite of your heart, I think. Alas, poor heart. If you
spite it for my sake, I will spite it for yours, for I will
never love that which my friend hates.

BENEDICK   Thou and I are too wise to woo peaceably.

BEATRICE   It appears not in this confession; there's not one wise   60
man among twenty that will praise himself.

BENEDICK   An old, an old instance, Beatrice, that lived in the
time of good neighbours. If a man do not erect in this
age his own tomb ere he dies, he shall live no longer
in monument than the bell rings and the widow
weeps.[154]

BEATRICE   And how long is that, think you?

BENEDICK   Question! Why, an hour in clamour and a quarter in
rheum. Therefore is it most expedient for the wise, if
Don Worm (his conscience)[155] find no impediment to   70
the contrary, to be the trumpet of his own virtues, as I

am to myself. So much for praising myself, who, I
myself will bear witness, is praiseworthy. And now tell
me, how doth your cousin?

BEATRICE   Very ill.

BENEDICK   And how do you?

BEATRICE   Very ill too.

BENEDICK   Serve God, love me, and mend. There will I leave you
too, for here comes one in haste.

Enter URSULA.

URSULA   Madam, you must come to your uncle. Yonder's old   80
coil at home: it is proved my Lady Hero hath been
falsely accused, the Prince and Claudio mightily abused,
and Don John is the author of all, who is fled and
gone. Will you come presently?

BEATRICE   Will you go hear this news, signior?

BENEDICK   I will live in thy heart, die in thy lap, and be buried in
thy eyes;[156] and moreover, I will go with thee to thy
uncle's.   [*Exeunt.*

SCENE 3.

Night. Before a monumental tomb in a churchyard.

Enter DON PEDRO, CLAUDIO, *and three or four* LORDS *holding tapers.*

CLAUDIO   Is this the monument of Leonato?

LORD 1   It is, my lord.
[*He reads from a scroll:*]
    Done to death by slanderous tongues
        Was the Hero that here lies.
    Death, in guerdon of her wrongs,
        Gives her fame which never dies:
    So the life that died with shame
    Lives in death with glorious fame.
                    [*He hangs the scroll on the tomb.*
    Hang thou there upon the tomb,
    Praising her when I am dumb.   10

CLAUDIO   Now, music, sound, and sing your solemn hymn.[157]

LORDS *sing:*   Pardon, goddess of the night,
                Those that slew thy virgin knight;
                For the which, with songs of woe,
                Round about her tomb they go.
                    Midnight, assist our moan,
                    Help us to sigh and groan,
                        Heavily, heavily.
                    Graves, yawn and yield your dead,
                    Till death be utterèd,   20
                        Heavily, heavily.
LORD 1   Now, unto thy bones, good night.
            Yearly will I do this rite.¹⁵⁸
D. PEDRO Good morrow, masters; put your torches out.
              The wolves have preyed; and look, the gentle day,
            Before the wheels of Phoebus, round about
            Dapples the drowsy east with spots of grey.¹⁵⁹
            Thanks to you all, and leave us. Fare you well.
CLAUDIO   Good morrow, masters; each his several way.
                                        [*Exeunt the lords.*
D. PEDRO Come, let us hence, and put on other weeds,   30
            And then to Leonato's we will go.
CLAUDIO   And Hymen now with luckier issue speed 's,
            Than this for whom we rendered up this woe!¹⁶⁰
                                              [*Exeunt.*

SCENE 4.

MUSICIANS *are present.*¹⁶¹ *The hall in Leonato's house.*

Enter LEONATO, ANTONIO, BENEDICK *and* FRIAR FRANCIS,
followed by HERO, BEATRICE, MARGARET
and URSULA, *who talk privately.*

FRIAR   Did I not tell you she was innocent?
LEONATO So are the Prince and Claudio, who accused her
              Upon the error that you heard debated;
              But Margaret was in some fault for this,
              Although against her will, as it appears

In the true course of all the question.[162]

ANTONIO   Well, I am glad that all things sort so well.

BENEDICK   And so am I, being else by faith enforced
           To call young Claudio to a reckoning for it.

LEONATO   [turns.] Well, daughter, and you gentlewomen all,   10
           Withdraw into a chamber by yourselves,
           And when I send for you, come hither masked.
                         [Exeunt Hero, Beatrice, Margaret and Ursula.
           The Prince and Claudio promised by this hour
           To visit me. You know your office, brother:
           You must be father to your brother's daughter,
           And give her to young Claudio.

ANTONIO   Which I will do with cónfirmed countenance.

BENEDICK   Friar, I must entreat your pains, I think.

FRIAR   To do what, signior?

BENEDICK   To bind me, or undo me; one of them.   20
           Signior Leonato, truth it is, good signior,
           Your niece regards me with an eye of favour.

LEONATO   That eye my daughter lent her. 'Tis most true.

BENEDICK   And I do with an eye of love requite her.

LEONATO   The sight whereof I think you had from me,
           From Claudio and the Prince. But what's your will?

BENEDICK   Your answer, sir, is enigmatical;
           But, for my will, my will is, your good will
           May stand with ours, this day to be conjoined
           In the state of honourable marriage,   30
           In which, good Friar, I shall desire your help.

LEONATO   My heart is with your liking.

FRIAR   And my help.
           Here comes the Prince and Claudio.[163]

           Enter DON PEDRO, CLAUDIO and two or three ATTENDANTS.

D. PEDRO   Good morrow to this fair assembly.

LEONATO   Good morrow, Prince, good morrow, Claudio:
           We here attend you. Are you yet determined
           Today to marry with my brother's daughter?

CLAUDIO   I'll hold my mind, were she an Ethiope.[164]

LEONATO   Call her forth, brother. Here's the Friar ready.
                                        [Exit Antonio.

D. PEDRO   Good morrow, Benedick. Why, what's the matter,   40
            That you have such a February face,
            So full of frost, of storm and cloudiness?
CLAUDIO   I think he thinks upon the savage bull.
            Tush, fear not, man, we'll tip thy horns with gold,
            And all Europa shall rejoice at thee,
            As once Europa did at lusty Jove,
            When he would play the noble beast in love.[165]
BENEDICK   Bull Jove, sir, had an amiable low;
            And some such strange bull leaped your father's cow,
            And got a calf in that same noble feat   50
            Much like to you, for you have just his bleat.[166]

                  Enter HERO, BEATRICE, MARGARET *and*
                  URSULA *(all masked), with* ANTONIO.

CLAUDIO   For this I owe you; here comes other reck'nings.
            Which is the lady I must seize upon?
ANTONIO   [*leading Hero:*] This same is she, and I do give you her.[167]
CLAUDIO   Why, then she's mine. Sweet, let me see your face.
LEONATO   No, that you shall not, till you take her hand
            Before this Friar, and swear to marry her.
CLAUDIO   Give me your hand before this holy Friar.
            I am your husband if you like of me.
HERO   [*unmasking:*] And when I lived, I was your other wife;   60
            And when you loved, you were my other husband.
CLAUDIO   Another Hero!
HERO   Nothing certainer.
            One Hero died defiled, but I do live;
            And surely as I live, I am a maid.
D. PEDRO   The former Hero! Hero that is dead!
LEONATO   She died, my lord, but whiles her slander lived.
FRIAR   All this amazement can I qualify.
            When after that the holy rites are ended,
            I'll tell you largely of fair Hero's death.
            Meantime, let wonder seem familiar,[168]   70
            And to the chapel let us presently.
BENEDICK   Soft and fair, Friar. Which is Beatrice?
BEATRICE   [*unmasking:*] I answer to that name. What is your will?
BENEDICK   Do not you love me?
BEATRICE   Why no, no more than reason.

BENEDICK　Why then your uncle and the Prince and Claudio
Have been deceived: they swore you did.[169]

BEATRICE　Do not you love me?

BENEDICK　　　　　　　　　Troth no, no more than reason.

BEATRICE　Why then my cousin, Margaret and Ursula
Are much deceived, for they did swear you did.

BENEDICK　They swore that you were almost sick for me.　　80

BEATRICE　They swore that you were well-nigh dead for me.

BENEDICK　'Tis no such matter. Then you do not love me?

BEATRICE　No, truly, but in friendly recompense.

LEONATO　Come, cousin, I am sure you love the gentleman.

CLAUDIO　And I'll be sworn upon't, that he loves her,
For here's a paper written in his hand,
A halting sonnet of his own pure brain,
Fashioned to Beatrice.

HERO　　　　　　　　And here's another,
Writ in my cousin's hand, stol'n from her pocket,
Containing her affection unto Benedick.　　90

BENEDICK　A miracle! Here's our own hands against our hearts.
Come, I will have thee; but, by this light, I take thee
for pity.

BEATRICE　I would not deny you; but, by this good day, I yield
upon great persuasion, and partly to save your life, for
I was told you were in a consumption.

BENEDICK　Peace, I will stop your mouth.[170]　　　[He kisses her.

D. PEDRO　How dost thou, Benedick the married man?

BENEDICK　I'll tell thee what, Prince: a college of wit-crackers
cannot flout me out of my humour. Dost thou think I　100
care for a satire or an epigram? No, if a man will be
beaten with brains, a shall wear nothing handsome
about him.[171] In brief, since I do purpose to marry, I
will think nothing to any purpose that the world can
say against it; and therefore never flout at me for what
I have said against it: for man is a giddy thing, and this
is my conclusion. For thy part, Claudio, I did think to
have beaten thee, but, in that thou art like to be my
kinsman, live unbruised, and love my cousin.

CLAUDIO　I had well hoped thou wouldst have denied Beatrice,　110
that I might have cudgelled thee out of thy single life,

to make thee a double-dealer; which out of question
thou wilt be, if my cousin do not look exceeding
narrowly to thee.[172]

BENEDICK Come, come, we are friends. Let's have a dance ere we
are married, that we may lighten our own hearts and
our wives' heels.

LEONATO We'll have dancing afterward.

BENEDICK *First*, of my word: therefore play, music. – Prince,
thou art sad; get thee a wife, get thee a wife: there is 120
no staff more reverend than one tipped with horn.[173]

Enter MESSENGER.

MESSEN. My lord, your brother John is ta'en in flight,
And brought with armèd men back to Messina.

BENEDICK Think not on him till tomorrow; I'll devise thee brave
punishments for him. – Strike up, pipers!

Music and dancing ensue.

In these notes, the abbreviations used include the following:

- Cf., cf.: *confer* (Latin): compare;
- e.g.: *exempli gratia* (Latin): for example;
- F: the First Folio (1623);
- i.e.: *id est*: that is;
- O.E.D.: *The Oxford English Dictionary* (2nd edition, 1989, and website);
- Q: the Quarto (1600);
- S.D.: stage-direction;
- S.P.: speech-prefix.

Biblical quotations are from the Geneva Bible (1560).
In the case of a pun or an ambiguity, the meanings are distinguished as (a) and (b), or as (a), (b) and (c).

1 *The title*:   The play's title, *Much Ado about Nothing*, probably has more than one meaning. The first and predominant meaning is 'A Great Fuss with No Real Cause', referring to the mistaken belief that Hero is unfaithful. The second may be 'A Great Fuss about a Vulva' (Hero's vulva) and is indicated by the following exchange in *Hamlet*, Act 3, scene 2: Hamlet remarks 'That's a fair thought to lie between maids' legs', Ophelia asks 'What is, my lord?', and he replies 'Nothing.' (In addition, 'thing' could occasionally signify 'penis', a signification perhaps invoked in *Much Ado*, 4.1.267.) Some editors and critics of *Much Ado about Nothing* have suggested that 'nothing' was pronounced 'noting' (rhyming with 'voting'), which yields the additional meaning, 'A Great Fuss about Taking Note or Observing'. This pronunciation is

not supported by *O.E.D.*; and Fausto Cercignani's *Shakespeare's Works and Elizabethan Pronunciation* (1981), pp. 137 and 329, argues that 'nothing' was pronounced 'no-thing' ('o' as in 'go' but 'th' as in 'thin'). Nevertheless, Shakespeare's Sonnet 20 appears to rhyme 'nothing' with 'doting', and *Much Ado about Nothing*, 2.3.52–5, seems to exploit an echo of 'noting' in 'nothing'. Its pronunciation may have varied.

2 (1.1, S.D.) ACT . . . Leonato's garden.:   There are no Act or scene divisions in Q; F specifies Act 1, scene 1, but thereafter only Act divisions. Those early texts do not specify locations at the openings of scenes. Editors often nominate locations which have been inferred from the dialogue and/or stage directions. Dialogue in Act 1, scene 2, indicates that initially the setting may be a garden with an orchard and a 'thick-pleached alley'.

3 (1.1, S.D.) Enter . . . MESSENGER.:   In Q, the S.D. is: '*Enter Leonato gouernour of Messina, Innogen his wife, Hero his daughter, and Beatrice his neece, with a messenger.*' F's direction is almost identical. At the opening of Act 2, the S.D. of Q (copied by F) again refers to Leonato's wife. She has no evident function in the play, so editors usually omit both references to her. Perhaps Shakespeare changed his mind about using her, or perhaps she is a relic of an earlier version of the play. I preserve her as evidence (with other textual features) that *Much Ado about Nothing* has survived only in an exploratory and unfinalised state. Shakespeare could have derived Innogen's name from Holinshed's *Chronicles*. The name 'Hero' derives from Greek legend: the classical Hero was a priestess whose lover, Leander, swam the Hellespont at night to visit her; but, one night, he drowned, and she subsequently committed suicide. At 4.1.99, Claudio refers to the legendary namesake.

4 (1.1.1) *Don Peter of Arragon*:   In Q, he is here 'don Peter of Arragon' (while F terms him '*Don Peter of Arragon*'), but after line 8 he becomes 'Don Pedro'.

5 (1.1.26) *Signior Mountanto*:   Her name for Benedick could mean 'Mister Aspirant' and 'Mister Thruster', the latter connoting experience both in fencing (*montante* being then Italian for an upward thrust with the sword) and in sexual matters (*montare* being Italian for 'to mount or copulate with',

referring to animals). In *Cymbeline*, Act 2, scene 4, Posthumus imagines that Iachimo, like a boar, 'mounted' Imogen.

6 (1.1.33–6) *He . . . birdbolt.*: 'He put up notices here in Messina to challenge Cupid at archery with the light long-distance arrow, and my uncle's Fool, reading the challenge, deputised for Cupid and challenged him with the birdbolt.' A birdbolt is a short blunt arrow to stun birds. (Perhaps the Fool knew that Benedick could find love close at hand, in Messina.)

7 (1.1.42–4) *You had . . . stomach.*: 'He has "done good service" only at the dining-table: you had stale food, and he has helped to eat it. He is a very bold emptier of a wooden dish: he has an excellent appetite for food (rather than for fighting).'

8 (1.1.66) *and he were,*: 'and', here and on some subsequent occasions, serves as a subordinating conjunction, equivalent to 'if'. Some editors render it as 'an', to avert confusion with 'and' used as a co-ordinating conjunction.

9 (1.1.72–4) *if . . . cured.*: 'if he has caught the Benedick disease (Benedick's company): the cure will cost Claudio a thousand pounds' — implying that before he tires of Benedick, the friendship will be costly to him. In 'ere a be cured', 'a' serves (as sometimes subsequently in the play) as a colloquial abbreviation of the pronoun 'he'. (In such cases, F sometimes substitutes 'he' for Q's 'a'.)

10 (S.D. after 1.1.79) *Enter . . . bastard').*: The Q and F stage-directions here include Balthasar, although he says nothing in the ensuing scene, and refer to Don John as '*Iohn the bastard*'.

11 (1.1.91–3) *Signior . . . herself.*: Leonato jestingly remarks that Innogen would have been safe from seduction, as Benedick was then only a child. Don Pedro comments that this remark fully reveals what kind of man Benedick is (a womaniser). Hero 'fathers herself' in that she resembles (and thus identifies) her father.

12 (1.1.119–20) *Well . . . yours.*: He implies that she is very good at repeating empty phrases. She responds that a bird which talks like herself is better than any dumb beast of his.

13 (1.1.132–3) *being . . . brother,*: 'now that you are reconciled to the Prince, your brother,'.

14 (1.1.156–60) *But speak . . . song?*:   'But do you say this with a
serious demeanour? Or are you acting like a trouble-maker
who asserts that Cupid, the blind love-god, is good at locating
hares, and that Vulcan, blacksmith to the gods, is actually an
exceptional carpenter? Come on: what musical key should I
adopt in order to harmonise with you?' ('Sad' often means
'serious' in this play.)

15 (1.1.170–74) *In faith . . . Sundays.*:   'Truly, doesn't the world
have one man who can wear a cap without being suspected of
being a cuckold? Shall I never see a sixty-year-old bachelor
again? Really, go away, if you must thrust your neck into a
yoke (like a paired ox), bear the imprint of it, and sigh
through Sundays (because you will no longer be free to enjoy
yourself then).' A cuckold, a man whose wife was unfaithful
to him, was said to grow horns (or a horn) from his head. A
cap would conceal them.

16 (S.D. after 1.1.174) Enter DON PEDRO.:   Q and F have '*Enter
don Pedro, Iohn the bastard.*': a faulty direction, as Don John
first hears in scene 3 of Claudio's intended marriage.

17 (1.1.186–8) *If . . . be so.*':   Claudio's ambiguous reply probably
means: 'If this were the case, it would be admitted.' To
criticise such evasiveness, Benedick then quotes a folk-tale in
which a murderous gentleman, Mr Fox, repeatedly denies
being a killer.

18 (1.1.208–10) *that I will . . . pardon me.*:   'women must excuse
me either from having a horn-call sounded in my forehead or
from hanging my horn in an invisible shoulder-belt'. A
'recheat' is a hunting-call played on a horn; a 'bugle' is also a
horn (originally made from the horn of the animal called the
bugle, the wild ox); and a 'baldric' is a belt, worn over one
shoulder and under the opposite arm, sometimes used to hold
a forester's horn. In short, Benedick declines marriage,
declaring that it would inevitably make him a cuckold. (Act
4, scene 3, of John Lyly's *Midas*, *c.* 1589, had previously
exploited the 'bugle, horn, cuckold's horn' association.)

19 (1.1.216–19) *Prove . . . Cupid.*:   'Prove' here means 'If you
can prove'. Lovers' sighs were supposed to deplete the blood,
and drinking was supposed to increase it. Lovers sometimes

composed or recited ballads. Brothels, like taverns, bore painted signs.

20 (1.1.222–4) *hang . . . Adam.*:   Apparently cats in baskets were sometimes used as targets by archers. (Here, 'bottle' is usually taken by editors to mean 'basket'.) This 'Adam' is probably Adam Bell, a legendary archer and outlaw.

21 (1.1.226) *'In time . . . yoke.'*:   proverbial, and popularised by Thomas Kyd's *The Spanish Tragedy*. A horning jest ensues.

22 (1.1.234–7) *Nay . . . hours.*:   Venice was notorious for libertinism and prostitution. Benedick says that only an earthquake, not the pangs of love, could make him tremble. '[Y]ou will temporize with the hours' means either 'You will only be postponing the inevitable' or 'You will become amenable in course of time'.

23 (1.1.242–9) *I commit . . . leave you.*:   Claudio and Don Pedro cap Benedick's 'so I commit you' by adding stock phrases from letters. Benedick, using metaphors from tailoring, says that they are in no position to mock him, as they abuse bits of language as much as he does. The 'body' is (a) the main part of a garment, or (b) a bodice; 'guards' are its decorations; 'basting' is temporary sewing, and 'old ends' are scraps of material as well as literary tags.

24 (1.1.269–70) *And I . . . have her.*:   These words are present in Q; but F, after 'And I will breake with her:', omits the rest.

25 (1.1.273) *That . . . complexion!*:   'who recognise a lover's woe by his (pale) appearance'. 'Complexion' could be pronounced tetrasyllabically ('com-plex-i-on') to preserve the metre.

26 (1.1.277) *The fairest . . . necessity.*:   'The best gift is the one that provides the essentials.'

27 (1.2, S.D.) *In . . . meeting.*:   The S.D. in Q is simply: '*Enter Leonato and an old man brother to Leonato.*' F's direction is substantially the same. The location may be a room or a hall.

28 (1.2.12–14) *if he . . . of it.*:   'if he found her in agreement, he meant to seize the opportunity, and immediately inform you of the matter.' To 'take time by the top' was proverbial. Opportunity was sometimes represented as a female figure ('*Occasio*'or 'Occasion') whose head was bald behind but bore

a forelock hanging over the forehead, to show that one should seize a chance as soon as it appears.

29 (1.2, S.D. after 21) Enter *ATTENDANTS*.:   Q and F have no S.D. here. The attendants may include the people indicated in lines 1–2, Antonio's son and a musician or two (though Antonio's son does not appear elsewhere). 'Cousin', a term used loosely, ranged in meaning from 'nephew' to 'dependant, member of the household'.

30 (1.3, S.D.) Outside Leonato's house.:   This location is conjectural. As usual, Q and F specify no location. Editors' suggestions include: 'A room in Leonato's house', 'the street', and 'a gallery in Leonato's house'.

31 (1.3.1) *What . . . lord?*:   'What the good-year . . . ?' is probably equivalent to 'What the devil is the matter . . . ?'

32 (1.3.8–9) *born . . . Saturn*:   People born when Saturn was prominent in the sky were thought to be 'saturnine': gloomy, melancholy and ill-willed (as is Saturninus in *Titus Andronicus*).

33 (1.3.14) *claw . . . humour.*:   'scratch nobody's back when he is in the mood for it'.

34 (1.3.26–8) *I am . . . clog*::   'I am trusted only when I am muzzled (when I can neither bark nor bite), and I have only as much liberty as an animal tied to a clog (a heavy wooden weight):'.

35 (1.3.47–9) *Being . . . conference.*:   'While I, employed as an air-scenter, was fumigating a stale-smelling room, the Prince and Claudio entered hand in hand, in earnest discussion.' Smelly rooms were scented by burning aromatic herbs, e.g. juniper. In the clause 'comes me the Prince and Claudio', the 'me' is an 'ethical dative', used here to give a colloquially personal quality.

36 (1.3.59–60) *would . . . mind!*:   'I wish the cook shared my view (for then he would poison their food)!'

37 (2.1, S.D.) A hall . . . house.:   Q and F do not specify a location. Editors usually propose a hall or great chamber in Leonato's house, though an alternative proposal is Leonato's garden.

38 (2.1.19–21) *Too . . . none.*: 'To be too ill-natured is worse
than being ill-natured, but that way I incur less from God, for
it is proverbially said that God gives an ill-natured cow short
horns (to reduce its power to do harm), whereas to a cow
which is too ill-natured he gives none at all (i.e., the woman
will not be given a husband, who would bear the cuckold's
horns).'

39 (2.1.33–4) *I will . . . hell.*: 'I will actually take sixpence in
advance payment from the bear-keeper (who keeps other
animals too) and lead his apes to hell.' She alludes to the
proverb, 'Old maids lead apes in hell'. (Apes were deemed
lustful.)

40 (2.1.40–42) *Saint . . . long.*:   St Peter is the gate-keeper of
heaven. 'As merry as the day is long' is proverbial.

41 (2.1.52–6) *Would . . . kindred.*:   In describing a man as 'a
piece of valiant dust', Beatrice recalls Genesis 2:7, in which
God makes Adam of 'dust of the grounde' (Geneva Bible).
'Marl' is clay. Leviticus 18:6 forbids sexual relationships with
one's 'kindred of . . . flesh'. Beatrice's joke is that since all
men and women are (in a sense) Adam's children, and siblings
are forbidden to marry, it would be sinful for her to marry.

42 (2.1.61–2) *there is . . . answer.*:   Beatrice recalls the proverb,
'There is measure in all things' (i.e. 'Moderation should be
sought'), and exploits the ambiguity of 'measure', which here
may mean not only 'moderation' but also 'tempo in music', 'a
dance' and 'a particular stately dance'. (The last sense emerges
at line 63.)

43 (2.1, S.D. after 71) Enter . . . BORACHIO.:   Q gives the S.D. as
'*Enter prince, Pedro, Claudio, and Benedicke, and Balthaser, or dumb
Iohn.*'; F gives: '*Enter Prince, Pedro, Claudio, and Benedicke, and
Balthasar, or dumbe Iohn, Maskers with a drum.*' Evidently '*dumb
Iohn*' is Don John. Line 146 is attributed by Q and F to
Borachio. In the Q speech-prefixes (copied by F), Margaret's
partner is identified both as Benedick and as Balthasar; I follow
other editors in identifying him only as Balthasar.

44 (2.1.81–2) *My visor . . . love.*:   Here the exchange of dialogue
forms a rhyming couplet in 'fourteeners' (lines of fourteen
syllables, each line having seven iambic feet). The legendary

Philemon, a peasant, gave hospitality in his thatched cottage to Jove (Jupiter), the supreme god. Don Pedro means: 'Although my visor (my mask or half-mask) may look ugly to you, think of it as the roof of Philemon's cottage: within that dwelling a wonderfully majestic being may be found.' Hero replies: 'In that case, your visor should be thatched' (perhaps indicating that he is bald).

45 (2.1.89–93) *God . . . answered.*:   When Balthasar says 'Amen' ('So be it') in response to her prayer for a good dancing-partner, he adopts the rôle of a parish clerk who leads the responses during an ecclesiastical service. Margaret then out-wits him by a prayer to which he cannot respond 'Amen'.

46 (2.1.110) *the . . .* Tales: *A Hundred Merry Tales* was a popular book of amusing but unsubtle anecdotes (some being crude and coarse) first published in 1526.

47 (2.1.117–18) *only . . . slanders.*:   'his only talent is for devising unbelievable slanders.'

48 (2.1.122–3) *I am . . . me.*:   'In the fleet' means metaphorically 'in the assembly of dancers', and she extends the naval phrasing in 'boarded' ('climbed aboard'), i.e. encountered, accosted.

49 (2.1.140) *you . . . love.*:   'you are a very dear friend of my brother.'

50 (2.1.155–8) *beauty . . . not.*:   'beauty is an enchantress whose charms make desire dissolve loyalty. Such an occurrence, which I did not suspect, has hourly proof.'

51 (2.1.163–7) *Even . . . Hero.*:   A willow garland (as Ophelia and Desdemona knew) was the symbol of a rejected lover. A lieutenant's sash was worn diagonally over the left shoulder and under the right arm.

52 (2.1.180–82) *I am . . . out.*:   The phrase 'the base (though bitter)', found in Q and F, is emended by some editors as 'the base and bitter' or 'the base, the bitter'. Benedick may mean: 'I do not have that reputation. Beatrice alone puts me into that low category (though causing me bitterness). That's how she describes me, as if her personal view were the general view.' (In this reading, 'disposition of ' is taken to mean 'allocation by'.)

53 (2.1, S.D. after 183) Enter . . . privately.: Q's stage-direction is: '*Enter the Prince, Hero, Leonato, John and Borachio, and Conrade.*' F gives: '*Enter Claudio and Beatrice, Leonato, Hero.*' As F probably represents staging practice, and as Don John, Borachio and Conrade say nothing subsequently in this scene (and their presence clutters the stage with an incongruous group), editors usually delete their names.

54 (2.1.185–6) *Lady . . . warren.*: His 'Lady Fame' derives from the Roman goddess Fama, who spreads rumours. '[A] lodge in a warren' may be (a) a hut in an enclosed area for breeding game, or (b) a form or burrow in an abode of hares or rabbits. Hares and rabbits were associated with melancholy.

55 (2.1.215–16) *a man . . . me.*: In archery, a man sometimes stood near the target, to signal the result.

56 (2.1.217–19) *if her breath . . . Star.*: 'if her breath were as terrible as her expressions, nobody could live near her, and she would infect everything, even as far as the North Star.' (The North Star was thought to be the most remote of the stars.)

57 (2.1.219–25) *I would . . . her,*: Before he transgressed by eating the forbidden fruit, Adam was given dominion over all that lives and grows on earth. The legendary Hercules became the slave of Queen Omphale of Lydia: she dressed him in women's clothes and made him undertake spinning. Benedick says that Beatrice would be worse: she would make Hercules turn the roasting-spit (like the lowest of kitchen menials) and would split his club to use as firewood. Ate was the Greek goddess of discord. Benedick wishes that some scholar, who would know the appropriate Latin formulations required for the ceremony of exorcism, could conjure Ate-Beatrice back to hell (because while she is on earth, hell is peaceful but earth is hellish).

58 (2.1.230–37) *Will . . . harpy.*: Rather than speak to Beatrice, Benedick would go to the remotest parts of the earth. 'Antipodes' were people whose feet were opposed to ours (because of the curvature of the earth) but who were sometimes located in Ethiopia. A 'tooth picker' is a tooth-pick. 'Prester John' was the legendary Christian ruler of a large remote realm sometimes identified as Ethiopia. 'The Great

Cham' was often identified with Kublai Khan, the Mongol emperor who completed the conquest of China. The Pigmies, too, were also described as oriental (e.g. by Sir John Mandeville). Harpies (depicted in Virgil's *Æneid*, Book 3) are voracious, noisy and filthy monsters, each having the face and torso of a woman but the wings and legs of a bird.

59 (2.1.244–7) *Indeed . . . lost it*.: 'Indeed, my lord, he did lend me his heart for a while, and I paid him interest on it: he gained twice as much love from me as he had ventured. Once previously (by St Mary!) he won my heart by false play; and therefore your Grace may well say I have lost it.'

60 (2.1.258–9) *civil as . . . complexion*.: 'Civil' (serious) leads to a pun on 'Seville' (then usually pronounced 'civil'), a type of orange. Yellow, as well as green, was deemed a colour of jealousy.

61 (2.1.266–7) *his Grace . . . to it*.: 'his Grace, Don Pedro, has made the match, and may the source of all grace, God, bless it by saying "So be it".'

62 (2.1.276–7) *poor . . . care*.: 'little jester, it takes the wind out of sorrow's sails.'

63 (2.1.280–82) *Good . . . husband'*.: 'Praise the Lord for marriage! Every one in the world goes that way but me, and I am too ugly for it, as if sun-darkened. I can only sit in a corner and yearn for a husband.' (A woman who was 'sun-burnt', in an era when a pale skin was fashionable, would be deemed unattractive. 'Heigh-ho for a husband!', sometimes meaning 'I wish I had a husband' or 'Go whistle for a husband', was proverbial.)

64 (2.1.295–6) *there . . . born*.: She perhaps recalls the superstitious notion that the sun danced on Easter Day.

65 (2.1.301) *melancholy element*: A person's temperament was thought to result from the mixture of the four bodily humours: blood, phlegm, choler and melancholy. These corresponded to the four elements: air, water, fire and earth.

66 (2.2.33–4) *cozened . . . maid)*.: 'deceived by a person who merely appears to be a virgin).'

67 (2.2.38) *Claudio*: If would seem more logical for her to say 'Borachio', thus confirming the apparent infidelity; but perhaps

Borachio plans to persuade Margaret to enter a rôle-playing assignation in which he pretends to be Claudio while she pretends to be Hero. (Some editors emend 'Claudio' as 'Borachio'.)

68 (2.3.5) *I am . . . sir.*:   The boy means: 'It's as good as done'; but Benedick pretends to take him literally. The boy never reappears, so the dialogue in lines 1–5 seems to be a pointless 'loose end'. In some stage-productions, the boy produces the book from his pocket as a silent rebuke to Benedick before making his exit; in others, he is deleted.

69 (2.3.12–14) *I have . . . pipe.*:   The drum and fife were military instruments. The tabor (small drum) and pipe (three-stopped whistle) were used at fairs and festivals, and were played by Fools.

70 (2.3.30–31) *noble . . . angel;*:   He puns on the names of gold coins, the 'noble' being worth one-third the value of a pound and the 'angel' (which depicted the archangel Michael) half the value of a pound. He may mean: (a) 'She must be noble, or I would not take her if I were paid an angel', or (b) 'She must be noble, or I shall be damned (rather than go to heaven) if I take her', or (c) 'She must be noble, or I shall not take her even if she be an angel.'

71 (2.3, S.D. after 34) *Enter . . . lute.*:   In Q, the S.D. is '*Enter prince, Leonato, Claudio, Musicke.*', followed, after six lines, by '*Enter Balthaser with musicke.*' In F, the S.D. is only '*Enter Prince, Leonato, Claudio, and Iacke Wilson.*', Jack Wilson being evidently the musician who acted Balthasar and played a stringed instrument (probably a lute).

72 (2.3.40) *We'll . . . pennyworth.*:   'We'll give the fox-cub more than he bargained for.' Q and F have 'kid-foxe', but some editors emend it as 'hid fox'.

73 (2.3.44–5) *It is . . . perfection.*:   'A constant characteristic of highly-skilled people is that they misrepresent their own accomplishment.'

74 (2.3.54–5) *Why . . . nothing!*:   'Why, these are truly cranky expressions – note notes, indeed, and nothing worth noting!' 'Crotchets' could mean both 'musical quarter-notes' and 'odd notions'. 'Nothing' probably had a long 'o' and thus made at least a vowel-rhyme with 'noting'.

75 (2.3.56–8) *Is it . . . done.*: 'Isn't it strange that sheep's guts (when pulled out to provide strings for a musical instrument) should have the power to draw men's souls from their bodies (in ecstatic enjoyment of music)? Well, when all is said and done, I put my money on the hunting-horn.' (He prefers hunting to balladry.)

76 (2.3.95) *Sits . . . corner?*: 'Is that the way the wind blows?'

77 (2.3.96–8) *By . . . thought.*:   Q and F punctuate the speech lightly, with a comma after both 'of it' and 'affection'. Consequently, the sense is ambiguous. I have emended the punctuation to select the following meaning: 'Truly, my lord, I do not know what to think of it, other than that she loves him with an intense attachment. It is beyond the endless range of thought (i.e. it surpasses belief).' The alternative meaning would be: 'Truly, my lord, I do not know what to think of it; but it is beyond the endless range of thought to believe that she loves him with an intense attachment.'

78 (2.3.180) *fear and trembling.*:   In Philippians 2:12, St Paul says that salvation should be attained 'with feare and trembling'.

79 (2.3.196–8) *The sport . . . matter.*:   'The fun will occur when each of them baselessly thinks the other madly in love.'

80 (2.3.233–5) *Yea . . . well.*:   'Yes, exactly as much pleasure as you could collect with a knife's point and use to choke a jackdaw. Have you no appetite for dinner? Farewell.' (Some editors emend the 'and choake a daw' of Q and F as 'and not choke a daw'.)

81 (2.3.241–2) *if I . . . picture.*:   'if I do not love her, I am a Jew (an infidel) and no Christian. I shall go to commission a miniature portrait of her (as a lover does).' There is probably an anti-Semitic implication that Jews are hard-hearted: cf. *The Merchant of Venice*, 4.1.78–80.

82 (3.1.4) *Ursley*:   Q has 'Vrsley' (i.e. 'Ursley'), an informal contraction of 'Ursula'. F has '*Vrsula*'.

83 (3.1.42) *To wish . . . affection,*:   The metre becomes regular if here 'affection' is pronounced tetrasyllabically ('aff–éc–she–òn'), though the word remains trisyllabic at line 55.

84 (3.1.55) *Nor . . . affection*:   'nor can she form any image or notion or love'.

85 (3.1.76–8) *press . . . inwardly::*   Suspects and malefactors were sometimes tortured or killed by means of weights gradually heaped on their chests. 'Fire that's closest kept burns most of all' was proverbial. A lover's sigh was supposed to make a little of his blood evaporate.

86 (3.1.101) *every day, tomorrow!::*   'every day, from tomorrow onwards'.

87 (3.1.104) *She's limed . . . you::*   Small birds were caught when they alighted on twigs which had been smeared with bird-lime, a gluey substance deriving from holly, mistletoe or other plants. Though Q has 'limed', F has 'tane' (meaning 'taken, caught').

88 (3.2.19–25) *I have . . . has it.:*   When Benedick claims to have toothache, Don Pedro tells him to have the tooth pulled out, and Benedick responds with the exclamation 'Hang it!' (equivalent to 'Curse it!'). Claudio says that the tooth must be hanged (perhaps noosed with a string) before it can be pulled, an allusion to the judicial punishment of hanging, drawing and quartering. Leonato alludes to the medical belief that toothache was caused by bodily fluids or small worms. In line 25, 'can' is a traditional emendation of the 'cannot' found there in Q and F.

89 (3.2.29–32) *or in . . . doublet.:*   The German wears baggy breeches, and the Spaniard wears a cape or cloak which conceals or replaces the customary jacket. F omits this passage, perhaps as a result of censorship.

90 (3.2.40–41) *the old . . . tennis-balls.:*   Tennis-balls were indeed stuffed with human hair.

91 (3.2.51–2) *Nay . . . stops.:*   'Furthermore, he has lost his enthusiasm for jesting, and prefers to play the lute or a wind-instrument.' (In *Hamlet*, for example, the 'stops' are the tuning-holes in a recorder.)

92 (3.2.58–60) *dies . . . upwards.:*   Claudio means that she is dying to marry Benedick. Don Pedro, perhaps recalling the bawdy sense of 'die' ('have an orgasm'), implies that her 'burial' will be in bed underneath Benedick.

93 (3.2.61–5) *Old . . . Beatrice.:*   This creates another of the play's inconsistencies, because in 5.4.21–30 Benedick appears

to broach the matter to Leonato for the first time. 'For my life' means 'I swear by my life'.

94 (3.2.97–8) *If you . . . wed her.*:   The punctuation of 'her then, tomorrow' is a traditional editorial emendation; Q and F place the comma after 'her'.

95 (3.3, S.D.) WATCHMEN: Watchmen, in Shakespeare's day, were local citizens chosen for nocturnal police duties. In the Q and F versions of this scene, the speech-prefixes for the watchmen are casually allocated, and sometimes no differentiation is indicated. Editors therefore try to effect a tidier arrangement, but results vary considerably.

96 (3.3.2–3) *salvation . . . soul.*:   Verges confuses 'salvation' with 'damnation'. The subsequent dialogue contains similar confusions.

97 (3.3.9) *constable?*:   Here, 'constable' means 'leader of the watch', since Dogberry is already the Master (or Head) Constable.

98 (3.3.13) *good name.*:   Coal brought by sea from Newcastle was noted for its high quality.

99 (3.3.53–4) *they . . . defiled.*:   Ecclesiasticus 13:1: 'He that toucheth pitch, shalbe defiled with it . . . '

100 (3.3.77–8) *And . . . me.*:   'If any important matter happens to arise, summon me.'

101 (3.3.107–8) *is nothing . . . man.*:   He means that the clothes are insignificant when compared to the man who wears them. Conrade takes him to mean that they do not matter to a man. (Borachio's drunken discourse suits his name, as *borracho* is Spanish for 'drunkard'.)

102 (3.3.122–6) *Pharaoh's . . . club?*:   The smoke-stained ('reechy') painting may have shown Pharaoh's army pursuing the Israelites (Exodus 14:23–8). Daniel defeated the corrupt priests of Bel (Baal) in the apocryphal 'Historie of Bel', verses 3–22. Hercules, the warrior-hero worshipped as a god, wielded a club. A 'codpiece', worn at the front of a man's breeches or hose, was a pouch for the genitals.

103 (3.3.150) *We . . . stand!*:   In Q and F, this speech is allocated to the first watchman; but, as the second watchman (Seacoal)

was appointed leader of the group, it should probably be allocated to him.

104 (3.3.158–60) *Masters . . . us.*:   In Q and F, all these words are allocated to Conrade. Clearly most of them belong to a watchman. By 'obey' he means 'oblige'.

105 (3.3.161–3) *We are . . . you.*:   'Commodity' means: (a) 'useful article' and (b) 'goods obtained from a usurer'; 'taken up of ' means: (a) 'arrested with the aid of ' and (b) 'received on credit for'; 'bills' are (a) 'long-handled weapons, e.g. halberds' and (b) 'bonds given as securities'; and 'in question' means: (a) 'sought after', (b) 'subject to legal proceedings', and (c) 'of questionable value'.

106 (3.4.18–20) *cuts . . . tinsel*:   The 'cuts' were slits to reveal the lining; 'down sleeves' were long sleeves to the wrists; 'side-sleeves' were loose and open, hanging from the shoulder. The 'bluish tinsel', a light-blue silk cloth with metallic threads, decorated either the hem of the skirt or the hem of a petticoat revealed beneath it.

107 (3.4.41–2) *Ye . . . barns.*:   'You (Margaret) will be promiscuous; and then, if your husband owns plenty of stables, you will ensure that he has barns' (punning on 'barns' meaning 'bairns', children). Margaret responds by calling this an 'illegitimate construction' (meaning both 'improper characterisation' and 'imputation that there may be illegitimate children') and spurning it.

108 (3.4.45–9) *By my . . . star.*:   'Hey-ho' (or 'Heigh-ho') could be a call to a hawk or horse, as well as a sigh for a husband. The noun 'ache' was pronounced 'aitch', hence Beatrice's pun on the letter 'H'. To 'turn Turk' meant 'to become a renegade'. Margaret means: 'If you, Beatrice, have not become a renegade (by welcoming love, after all), nothing is reliable.' (The 'star' is the Pole Star, a reliable guide to navigators.)

109 (3.4.54–8) *I am . . . left it.*:   Beatrice says she can't smell the gloves because she is 'stuffed', nasally congested by a cold in the head. Margaret exclaims 'A maid and stuffed!', meaning 'A virgin and yet pregnant!'. '[C]atching of cold' may punningly mean 'trapping of the woman who was embraced',

as a person 'colled' was a person embraced. Beatrice's phrase 'professed apprehension' means 'been a professional wit'. and Margaret's 'left it' means 'left the profession' (i.e. ceased to be witty).

110 (3.4.62–3) *Get you . . . qualm.*:   *Carduus benedictus* (also termed *Cnicus benedictus*, 'blessed thistle' or 'holy thistle') was regarded as a panacea, and here the term offers a near-pun on the name 'Benedick' (of which the Lain form was 'Benedictus', meaning 'Blessed'). A 'qualm' was a sudden faintness or nausea.

111 (3.4.75–6) *in despite . . . grudging,*:   'although he is now in love, it doesn't impair his appetite;' (i.e., he accepts his lot and is none the worse for it).

112 (3.4.80) *Not . . . gallop.*:   (a) 'Not a rapid canter (a taught pace).'; (b) 'No run of falsehood.'

113 (3.5.2–3) *confidence . . . nearly.*:   By 'confidence' and 'decerns' he means 'conference' and 'concerns'.

114 (3.5.14) *Comparisons . . . Verges.*:   By 'odorous' he means 'odious'. '*Palabras*' abbreviates the Spanish phrase '*pocas palabras*' ('few words').

115 (3.5.16–19) *It pleases . . . Worship.*:   Dogberry confuses 'tedious' with some word meaning 'rich'. (In line 22, he confuses 'exclamation' with 'acclamation'.)

116 (3.5.27–8) *excepting . . . presence.*:   He means 'with all due respect to your worthy self.', but he confuses 'respecting' and 'excepting'.

117 (3.5.41–2) *comprehended . . . persons,*:   He means 'apprehended two suspicious persons,'.

118 (3.5.51) *Francis Seacoal,*:   Some editors consider this to be Shakespeare's error for 'George Seacoal' (see 3.3.10); others think that there are two different Seacoals.

119 (3.5.56–8) *non-come . . . gaol.*:   'Non-come' may be Dogberry's confusion of 'nonplus' (perplexity) with 'non-compos' (from the Latin '*non compos mentis*', i.e. 'not of sound mind'). 'Excommunication' is his error for 'examination'.

120 (4.1.11–13) *If either . . . utter it.*:   The marriage service in *The Book of Common Prayer* (1595) includes: 'I require and charge

you . . . that if either of you doe know any impediment, why ye may not bee lawfully ioyned together in Matrimony, that ye confesse it.'

121 (4.1.20–21) *Interjections? . . . he!'*:   Benedick echoes William Lily's *Short Introduction of Grammar*: 'An Interiection . . . betokeneth a sudden passion of the minde . . . Some are of . . . Laughing: as Ha ha he.' (1597 text.)

122 (4.1.55) *Out . . . seeming!*:   This means (a) 'I condemn you, Hero, for deception!' or (b) 'I condemn you, deceptive appearance!'.

123 (4.1.143–4) *Sir . . . say.*:   In Q and F, this speech is set as prose.

124 (4.1.154–8) *Hear . . . apparitions*:   In Q and F, the counter-parts to the present lines 154–7 are set as prose (originally, in Q, to save space on the page). To preserve the metre of line 158, 'apparitions' can be pronounced as a five-syllabled word (cf. 'ostentation' in line 204). '[C]ourse of fortune' and 'By noting of' mean 'fortuitous turn of events' and (possibly) 'because I have been attentively observing'.

125 (4.1.165–6) *Which . . . book;*:   'which confirm by experience the lessons of my reading;'.

126 (4.1.230) *If . . . liver,*:   'if ever love commanded the interest of his liver,'. (The liver was supposedly the seat of the passions, including the passion of love.)

127 (4.1.233–8) *success . . . infamy.*:   'what follows will make the outcome better than any likelihood I can now foretell. But, should all my other plans miscarry, the assumption that the lady is dead will quieten the scandal of her shame.'

128 (4.1.251) *For . . . cure.*:   'because they take unusual steps to elicit the cure of unusual wounds': a counterpart to the proverb, 'A desperate disease must have a desperate remedy'.

129 (4.2, S.D.) DOGBERRY, VERGES: In the Q and F versions of this scene, Dogberry's lines are usually allocated to 'Kemp' (i.e. Will Kemp, the comic actor), while Verges' are allocated to 'Cowley' or 'Couley' (Richard Cowley, another actor).

130 (4.2.63) *Let . . . coxcomb.*:   Q attributes to 'Couley' the words 'Let them be in the hands of Coxcombe.' F attributes

to 'Sex.', the Sexton, the words 'Let them be in the hands of *Coxcombe.*' Editors often give the first six words to Verges and the last two words (emended as 'Off, coxcomb!') to Conrade. This edition minimises emendation by giving all eight to Conrade, so that he appears to be mocking Dogberry's command that the prisoners be 'opinioned' (pinioned). The typesetter of Q may have confused 'Con', an abbreviation of 'Conrade', with 'Cou', an abbreviation of 'Couley'. (Conrade's speech at line 67 is attributed to Couley by Q and F, which confirms the likelihood of this confusion; and there, too, he gives a command and an insult.) 'Coxcomb' means 'fool', as a professional 'Fool' or jester would wear a hat crested with a strip of red cloth resembling a cock's comb.

131 (5.1.15–16) *If . . . groan;*:   These lines have given rise to a diversity of interpretations. The text in Q and F is: 'If such a one will smile and stroke his beard, / And sorrow, wagge, crie hem, when he should grone,'. A plausible reading is: 'If such a person will smile and stroke his beard (like one about to make a speech) while being sorrowful, or play the fool and cry "hem" (like a drinker) when groaning would be appropriate;'. Some editors emend the opening of line 16 as 'Bid sorrow wag, cry "Hem",' (meaning 'Tell sorrow to go away, and cry "Hem" like an orator'). In other works by Shakespeare, the cry 'Hem' is variously a prelude to a speech and a call by a drinker in a tavern.

132 (5.1.17–19) *make . . . patience.*:   The words 'make misfortune drunk / With candle-wasters' probably mean 'drown his sorrows with other people who stay up late at night (in revelry)'. An alternative is: 'stupefy misfortune with lore culled by bookworms'. In line 19, 'patience' is metrically trisyllabic.

133 (5.1.37–8) *However . . . sufferance.*:   These ambiguous words may mean: 'even if they have written as if they were gods, by attempting to relegate the power of chance and suffering.'

134 (5.1.82) *Win . . . answer me.*:   'When I'm beaten, then I'll submit; let him first accept my challenge.' ('Win it and wear it' is proverbial for 'Gain it and keep it'.)

135 (5.1.106–8) *My lord . . . it.*:   Line 106 is metrically regular if 'hear' be pronounced disyllabically ('*he*-ar'), as in *The Comedy*

of Errors, 5.1.26. Shakespeare may have intended the words from 'I will be heard' to 'smart for it.' to be deleted, as Q and F mark an exeunt for Leonato and Antonio at the end of line 107.

136 (5.1.114–15) *We . . . teeth*.: 'We came near to having our noses bitten off by two old toothless men.' *O.E.D.* allows 'had liked' as an alternative to the more customary form, 'had like'.

137 (5.1.127–8) *I will . . . us*.: 'I will ask you to draw forth your wit, just as we ask minstrels to draw their instruments from their cases (or to draw their bows across the strings), in order to give us pleasure.'

138 (5.1.142–7) *[quietly . . . cheer*.: The directions '*[quietly:]*' and '*[Loudly:]*' are editorial inferences from the dialogue, since Don Pedro does not hear the substance of the challenge but does hear what he assumes to be an invitation to a feast. Claudio's response to Benedick means: 'Good: I will meet you in order to have some amusement'; but 'good cheer' could also mean 'good food'.

139 (5.1.149–51) *he hath . . . too?*: Speaking metaphorically, so that Don Pedro will think that a feast is still the topic, Claudio mocks Benedick by saying that he (Claudio) has been challenged to wound (carve) a fool (calf 's-head), an impotent idiot (capon) and a gullible dolt (woodcock).

140 (5.1.158) *'a wise gentleman'*;: ' "a clever devil" ';'. (Cf. 'The Prince of Darkness is a gentleman': *King Lear*, 3.4.136.)

141 (5.1.170–71) *God . . . garden*.: Genesis 3:8–13 says that God, walking in the Garden of Eden, found Adam and Eve, who were hiding. Don Pedro hints that Benedick (in Act 2, scene 3) was observed when he thought himself concealed.

142 (5.1.172–5) *But when . . . man'?*: Don Pedro and Claudio mock Benedick's assertion (at 1.1.227–32) that if he ever married, bull's horns (to denote a cuckold) should be set on his head, and beneath his picture should appear the caption 'Here you may see Benedick the married man.'

143 (5.1.176–9) *Fare . . . not*.: The term 'boy' (for Count Claudio) expresses contempt. A 'gossip-like' humour is that of old

chatterers. Benedick says that the jokes they crack are as harmless as braggarts' swords (for the boasters break swords harmlessly to claim later that they were broken in combat).

144 (5.1.194–5) *Pluck . . . sad.*: 'Pull yourself together, heart, and be serious.'

145 (5.1, S.D. after 195) Enter . . . BORACHIO.: Q places the direction ('*Enter Constables, Conrade, and Borachio.*') after the present line 191; so does F (though specifying '*Constable*', not '*Constables*'.)

146 (5.1.213) *one . . . suited.*: 'one idea dressed up in several different ways.'

147 (5.1.269) *Can . . . invention,*: 'can create anything from your sad imagination,'. Metrically, 'invention' has four syllables here.

148 (5.1.276) *she alone . . . us.*: Like Leonato's wife, Antonio's son (mentioned at 1.2.1) has vanished.

149 (5.1.303) *God . . . foundation!*: one of the blessings uttered by people who received alms, especially at some religious establishment.

150 (5.2.4–7) *In so . . . stairs?*: He puns on 'style', meaning both a literary style and a rural stile. She comments that if no man will 'come over' her (surmount her sexually), she may always have to remain an unmarried servant, stationed 'below stairs'.

151 (5.2.13–18) *I give . . . come.*: Benedick's 'I give thee the bucklers' means 'I surrender; I give up'. A buckler is a small round shield. Margaret suggests that women already have 'bucklers' (perhaps meaning 'bellies') and would welcome 'swords' (perhaps implying 'penises'). Benedick comments that bucklers sometimes have spikes ('pikes') inserted into them 'with a vice' (possibly meaning both 'by screwing' and 'in course of sexual vice, e.g. lechery'), and that spikes offer perils to virgins ('maids'). Finally, Margaret's reference to 'Beatrice . . . , who I think hath legs', capped by Benedick's 'And therefore will come', may refer to a jocular question and answer of the time: 'How came you hither?' 'On my legs.'

152 (5.2.19–22) *The god . . . deserve*: This is a version of the opening of a love-song (printed in 1562) by William Elderton.

The words 'knows me, / How pitiful I deserve', which might strainedly mean 'knows how much I deserve pitying treatment (by the lady)', are taken by Benedick to mean 'knows that I deserve pitifully little'. In a full text of the song, the equivalent part reads '[The gods] knowe me, / how sorrofull I do serue', though later the lover requests 'some pitty whan I deserue'.

153 (5.2.23–33) *Leander . . . terms.*:   Leander swam the Hellespont to meet Hero, and Troilus employed Pandarus as go-between when wooing Cressida. A 'quondam carpet-monger' is an old-time ladies'-man, one who haunted women's carpeted chambers and boudoirs. 'Verse' derives from the Latin *vertere*, to turn; so Benedick wittily declares that lovers commemorated in verse have had a smooth time compared with himself, turned topsy-turvy by love. The rhymes or 'endings' that he imagines are 'ominous' because they suggest a cuckolded husband ('horn', 'fool') whose wife may produce another man's baby. A 'rhyming planet' might be Venus or the moon, since both were cited in amatory poems. 'Festival terms' would be terms of love-poetry, since love-ballads were sold at festivals (as is shown by Autolycus in *The Winter's Tale*).

154 (5.2.60–66) *It appears . . . weeps.*:   Beatrice comments: 'If you were wise, you would not have declared yourself so, since self-praise is not a characteristic of wise men.' Benedick then (recalling the proverb 'He has ill neighbours that is fain to praise himself ') says that her maxim ('instance') is out of date; today a man must commend himself, otherwise he will be soon forgotten.

155 (5.2.70) *Don . . . conscience)*:   The 'worm of conscience' is a traditional notion, probably deriving from Isaiah 66:24 and Mark 9:44, 46, 48.

156 (5.2.86-7) *die . . . eyes;*:   'Dic' could mean 'have an orgasm'. He will be 'buried in her eyes' when she closes her eyes in which he is reflected.

157 (5.3.3–11) *Done . . . hymn.*:   I follow Q and F, which allocate to a lord the recitation and to Claudio line 11. Some editors prefer to allocate the recitation to Claudio.

158 (5.3.12–23) *Pardon . . . rite.*:   Q and F do not have an identifying speech-prefix for the song, and they allocate to a lord
the couplet given here at lines 22–3. Some editors allocate
the song to Balthasar (though Q and F do not specify his
presence in this scene) and the couplet to Claudio. The
'goddess of the night' is Diana, deity of the moon and
chastity; Hero is her 'virgin knight' (virginal votaress).
'Heavily' means 'sadly'. Lines 19–20 probably mean: 'Graves,
open wide and release your dead occupants until all of them
have been emitted (to augment the gloom of the occasion)'.
Some editors, however, take 'Till death be utterèd' to mean
(a) 'Until death be driven out (at the Resurrection)'; or (b)
'Until death be fully expressed (by the lamentation)'. Line 22
here follows Q's 'Heauily heauily' and not F's '*heauenly,
heauenly*'.

159 (5.3.25–7) *the gentle . . . grey.*:   '[T]he wheels of Phoebus' are
the wheels of the chariot of Phoebus Apollo, the sun-god.
(The scene's transition from midnight to daybreak is even
swifter than in *Hamlet*, Act 1, scene 1.)

160 (5.3.32–3) *And Hymen . . . woe!*:   'And may Hymen bless us
so that the forthcoming marriage has a luckier outcome than
befell Hero, for whom we have offered up this lamentation!'
Hymen is the classical god of marriage.

161 (5.4, S.D) *MUSICIANS* are present.:   Q and F have no S.D.
specifying musicians in this scene, but musicians are required
by the concluding dialogues.

162 (5.4.6) *In . . . question.*:   Trisyllabic pronunciation of 'question' (as of 'marriage' in line 30) balances the metre.

163 (5.4.32–3) *And . . . Claudio.*:   'And my help' means 'And so
is my help'. Line 33 is present in Q but absent from F.

164 (5.4.38) *I'll . . . Ethiope.*:   Ethiopians were regarded as black-
skinned, and were therefore (in a tradition of racial prejudice)
sometimes deemed ugly.

165 (5.4.43–7) *I think . . . love.*:   In 1.1.227–9 and 5.1.172–5, the
joke was that Benedick, if married, would resemble a bull, for
he would wear the cuckold's horns. Claudio says that the
married Benedick would be consoled by gold provided by
Claudio and presumably Don Pedro. In line 45, 'Europa'

means 'Europe'. In line 46, the allusion is to the beautiful princess, Europa, whom lustful Jove (Jupiter), having assumed the form of a bull, carried on his back to Crete.

166 (5.4.48–51) *Bull . . . bleat.*: Benedick says that Claudio, who foolishly bleats like a bull-calf, must be the illegitimate offspring of his mother ('your father's cow') and a stranger (a 'strange bull'). 'Amiable' here means 'amorous'; 'calf' could mean 'dolt' or 'simpleton'.

167 (5.4.54) *This . . . her.*: Q and F allocate this speech to Leonato. Antonio, however, is ostensibly the bride's father, and has just entered with her, so numerous editors allocate these words (and sometimes lines 56–7) to Antonio.

168 (5.4.70) *let . . . familiar,*: 'let the marvellous seem ordinary,'.

169 (5.4.76) *Have . . . did.*: Some editors emend the line to regularise the metre (e.g. as 'Have been deceivèd, for they swore you did.'), but regularity is already provided by the auditory overflow of 'io' from the end of the previous line.

170 (5.4.96–7) *in a . . . mouth.*: '[I]n a consumption' could mean (a) 'suffering from a wasting disease' (such as pulmonary tuberculosis, in modern terms) and (b) 'being consumed by love sickness'. Q and F wrongly allocate line 97 to Leonato instead of Benedick.

171 (5.4.101–3) *No . . . him.*: 'No; a man who can be defeated by mockery will never wear any handsome clothes (for fear that they may attract ridicule).'

172 (5.4.111–14) *I might . . . thee.*: By 'a double-dealer', Claudio first means (a) a married man (one of a double) and (b) a turncoat, forswearing bachelorhood. Then he suggests that in marriage, if Beatrice should fail to keep close watch, Benedick will prove unfaithful (a double-crosser).

173 (5.4.120–21) *there is . . . horn.*: 'A horn-tipped staff of office is particularly respected, so you should enter marriage, which will make you a horn-topped cuckold.'

GLOSSARY

Where a pun or an ambiguity occurs, the meanings are distinguished as (a) and (b), or (a), (b) and (c), etc. Otherwise, alternative meanings are distinguished as (i) and (ii), or as (i), (ii) and (iii), etc. Abbreviations include the following: adj., adjective; adv., adverb; cf., compare; conj., conjunction; Fr., French; *O.E.D.*, *Oxford English Dictionary*; vb., verb.

a (as pronoun, as at 1.1.74, 2.1.15, 2.3.159, 178, 3.2.36, 44, etc.): he.

a (as preposition): in; **a God's name**: in God's name; **a mornings**: in the mornings.

abused: deceived.

accident: occurrence.

accordant: willing.

achiever: victor.

Adam: (i: 1.1.224:) probably Adam Bell, an outlawed archer; (ii: 2.1.55:) the biblical Adam, the first man.

advertisement: advice.

afeard: afraid.

affect: 1.1.256: (a) love; (b) like; (c) aim at.

agate: tiny figure in an agate seal-ring

aim: **aim better at me**: appraise me better.

allegiance: 3.3.5: (error for) disloyalty.

all is one: it makes no difference.

alms: **an alms to**: charity to.

amble: proceed at an easy pace.

'Amen': 'So be it.'

amiable: amorous.

ancient: experienced; **ancientry**: tradition.

and (as subordinating conj., e.g. at 1.1.66, 117, 164, 172, 2.3.78, 148, etc.): if; **and if**: 5.1.167: if.

angel: 2.3.31: (a) heavenly angel; (b) gold coin worth ten shillings.

answer: 2.1.204: match; **answer my mind**: match my wishes.

antic (noun): grotesque figure.

anticly: grotesquely.

Antipodes: people so distant that their feet seem opposed to ours.

appoint: arrange for.

apprehend: 2.1.69: (a) appraise; (b) comprehend.

apprehension: quickness of wit.

approve: prove.

arbour: bower of trees or climbing plants.

argument: (i: 1.1.221, 2.3.11:) topic; (ii: 2.3.51:) argument; (iii: 2.3.213:) evidence; (iv: 3.1.96:) rhetorical skill.

Arragon: Aragon.

arrant: outright, utter.

arras: tapestry hanging along a wall.

aspitious: (error for) suspicious.

assurance: certainty.

Ate: goddess of discord.

athwart: against.

bachelor: 2.1.41: unmarried male or female.

backward: spell him backward: completely misrepresent him.

badge of bitterness: show of grief.

baldric: belt worn over one shoulder and under the other.

banquet: dessert with fruit and wine.

basted on: loosely attached.

bate: abate, diminish.

bear'ard: bearward or bear-herd: bear-keeper.

bear in hand: deceive, delude; **bear it coldly**: remain cool.

Beatrice: 'She who blesses'.

Bel: Baal, a Babylonian god.

belie: slander.

bend (vb.): direct.

Benedick (from Latin *benedictus*): 'Blessed'.

bent: inclination, commitment; **bent of**: devotion to.

beshrew: curse.

betroth: pledge to marry.

bill (noun): (i: 1.1.33:) notice; (ii: 3.3.39:) long-handled weapon topped with a blade or axe-head; (iii: 3.3.162: a) long-handled weapon; (b) bond given as security.

birdbolt: short blunt arrow.

birlady: by Our Lady (the Virgin Mary).

birth: 2.1.142: hereditary nobility.

black: 3.1.63: dark in complexion.

blazon: description.

block: (i: 1.1.64: a) mould for hat; (b) blockhead; (ii: 2.1.209:) chopping-block.

blood: (i: 1.3.23:) disposition; (ii: 2.1.156, 2.3.153:) passion.

bloom of lustihood: glowing vigour.

blot (noun): blotch.

blown: 4.1.57: fully opened.

blunt: 3.5.9: (error for) sharp.

board (vb.): 2.1.122: (a) climb aboard; (b) accost.

bode: portend.

bold: be bold with: presume to ask.

books: in your books: 1.1.65–6: (a) in your good books, liked by you; (b) among your books.

Borachio (from Spanish *borracho*): 'Drunkard'.

bosom: in her bosom: privately.

bottle: 1.1.222: (perhaps) basket.

bout: round, turn; **walk a bout:** join the circuit of a dance.

bower. shady enclosure, often foliaged, in a garden.

brave: fine.

break: break jests: crack jokes; **break to:** broach the matter; **break with:** inform.

breathing (noun): breathing-space, interval.

broken: 2.3.216: inflicted.

brother: sworn brother: brother-in-arms, pledged to aid his comrade.

brow: sad brow: grave demeanour.

buckler: 5.2.14–16: (a) small round shield; (b) belly; **give thee the bucklers:** admit defeat by you.

burden: 3.4.39: (a) bass part; (b) weight of a man.

burglary: 4.2.45: (error for) perjury.

but: 2.1.36, 3.2.1: only.

calf: 3.3.65: fool.

candle-waster: 5.1.18: (a) reveller; (b) bookworm.

canker: 1.3.22: dog-rose: wild rose.

capon: castrated cock.

Carduus benedictus: 'blessed thistle' or 'holy thistle', a plant with healing powers.

career: gallop or charge in a tournament; **career of his humour:** progress of his inclination; **in the career:** in its onrush.

carpet-monger: ladies'-man.

carriage: fashion a carriage: compose an attitude.

carried. managed.

carving the fashion: designing.

catch (vb.): 5.2.9: snatch, snap.

catechizing: formalised questioning.

censure (vb.): estimate, regard.

Cham: Great Cham: Great Ruler (e.g. the Emperor of Mongolia and/or China).

chance (vb.): happen.

change: 4.1.182: exchange.

charge (noun): (i: 1.1.87:) burden; (ii. 3.3.7.) instruction in duties.

charge (vb.): 5.1.133: (a) aim; (b) impel.

cheapen: bargain for.

cheer, good cheer: 1.3.58, 5.1.147: (a) pleasure; (b) good food.

chid: complained.

cinque-pace (from Fr. but pronounced 'sink-apace'): (i: 2.1.64) lively dance;

(ii: 2.1.68: a) lively dance; (b) rapid decline.

circumstances shortened: reducing the details.

civet: musky perfume.

civil: 2.1.258: (a) polite; (b) of Seville.

clap's into: 3.4.39: (a) let's perform; (b) start us by clapping the rhythm of.

claw: 1.3.14: (a) stroke, soothe; (b) flatter.

codpiece: pouch for genitals, at the front of a man's breeches or hose.

cog: cheat.

coil: hubbub.

cold: catch cold: 3.4.55: (a) catch a cold in the head; (b) trap the 'colled' (woman embraced).

coldly: 3.2.112: coolly, calmly.

Comfect: Count Comfect: Count Candy.

committed: 5.1.211: arrested.

commodity: 3.3.161: (a) useful article; (b) goods obtained from a usurer.

comparison: break a comparison: vainly make a mocking analogy.

complement: formal civility.

complexion: facial appearance.

comprehend: 3.5.41–2: (error for) apprehend.

conceit: idea.

condition: ill conditions: bad qualities.

conference: conversation.

confidence: 3.5.2: (error for) conference.

confirmed: 2.1.333: (a) firm; (b) proven; **confirmed countenance:** straight face.

conjecture: distrust, suspicion.

conjure: exorcise: send back to Hell.

consumption: 5.4.96: (a) wasting disease; (b) love-sickness.

contemptible: contemptuous.

continuer: so good a continuer: had equal stamina.

controlment: restraint.

conveyance: dexterity.

correct (vb.): punish.

couchèd: hidden.

couch upon: lie on.

counsel: 2.3.186: (a) advice; (b) reflections.

count: 4.1.311: (a) account; (b) tale; (c) count (title).

County: Count.

cousin: (i: 1.2.1:) nephew; (ii: 1.2.22: a) kinsman; (b) dependant; (iii: 2.1.45:) cousin.

coverture: bower.

coxcomb: fool.

coy: disdainful.

coz: cousin.

cozen: cheat.

cross (vb.): stop, thwart; (adv.): **broke cross:** snapped in the middle.

crossness: contrariness.

crotchet: 2.3.54: (a) quarter-note; (b) odd notion.

cry: cry shame: 4.1.119:
(a) invoke shame; (b) shout
'Shame . . . '; I cry you
mercy: I beg your pardon.
cuckold: man whose wife is
unfaithful.
cuckold's horns: horns which
supposedly appear on a
cuckold's head.
Cupid: god of love, often
depicted as a blind boy-archer.
curiously: dextrously.
curst: ill-tempered, spiteful.
curtsies: 4.1.313: (a) curtsies,
formal obeisances;
(b) courteous manners.
cuts: 3.4.18: ornamental slashes
in outer layer of a garment.
daff: thrust aside.
daw: jackdaw.
dear: (i: 1.1.109:) valuable;
(ii: 4.1.326:) costly.
decern: (error for) concern.
decreed: determined.
defend: 2.1.79, 4.2.18: forbid.
deformed: 3.3.113: deforming.
deprave: defame, vilify.
despite: in the despite of: by
despising; only by despite:
merely to spite.
Dian: Diana, goddess of the
moon and chastity.
die: 5.2.86: have an orgasm.
difference: distinction.
discover: reveal.
dissembly: (error for) assembly.
divinity: theological knowledge.
division: arrangement.
doctor: learnèd man.

Dogberry: surname from
'dogberry', the fruit of the
dogwood (wild cornel) bush.
dotage: doting.
double-dealer: 5.4.112:
(a) married man;
(b) renegade; (c) adulterer.
doublet: close-fitting jacket.
drift: scheme.
drovier: 2.1.169: (a) cattle-
driver; (b) cattle-dealer.
dry hand: hand with the
dryness of old age.
ducat: coin of gold or silver.
dumb-show: speechless
entertainment.
dumps: 2.3.68: (a) sad moods;
(b) sad melodies.
earnest: in earnest of: in
advance payment for.
ecstasy: madness.
effest: 4.2.31: (a, perhaps)
Dogberry's confusion of
'aptest' and 'deftest';
(b, perhaps) misprint of
'deftest'; (c, perhaps) most
convenient (O.E.D.).
ends: old ends: 1.1.249–50:
(a) clichés, literary tags;
(b) tailor's scraps.
engaged: pledged.
enraged: 2.3.97: inflamed,
intense.
epithet: expression.
estimation: reputation.
Ethiope: Ethiopian, deemed
black-skinned.
Europa: (i: 5.4.45:) Europe;
(ii: 5.4.46:) Princess Europa.

even (adj.): 4.1.262: easy.
event: outcome.
ever: always.
exceeds: 3.3.16: is outstanding.
excepting: 3.5.27: (error for) respecting.
exclamation: 3.5.22: (error for) acclamation.
excommunication: 3.5.57: (error for) examination.
exeunt: they go out.
exhibition: (error for) commission.
exit: he or she goes out.
experimental seal: empirical proof.
fain: gladly.
fair: beautiful; fair-faced: fair-skinned.
faith (1.1.63, 2.1.156, 5.4.8): pledged loyalty.
false gallop: 3.4.80: (a) taught canter; (b) run of falsehood.
fancy: (i: 3.2.27–8: a) love; (b) capricious attraction; (ii: 3.2.95:) sexual preference; fancy to: love for.
fashioned to: addressed to.
fashion-monging: 5.1.94: (a) fashion-following; (b) fashion-trafficking.
father: fathers herself: 1.1.93: resembles (and thus identifies) her father.
favour: 2.1.79, 3.3.17: face.
February face: gloomy and hostile face.
fence: nice fence: stylish sword-fencing.

fetch in: 1.1.192: deceive.
fife: small flute.
fine (noun): 1.1.212: conclusion.
finer: go the finer: wear finer clothes.
five wits: five mental faculties.
flat: 2.1.193: outright.
fleer: sneer.
fleet: in the fleet: 2.1.122: (a) among the dancers; (b) in the navy.
flight: at the flight: at long-distance archery using a light arrow.
flout (vb.): mock; flouting (adj.): mocking; flouting Jack: mocking rogue; flout old ends: 1.1.247–8: (a) abuse epistolary clichés; (b) abuse tailor's scraps.
flow: 4.1.247: (a) dissolve; (b) weep copiously.
foil (noun): sword with blunted tip.
foining fence: thrusting style of sword-fencing.
Fool: jester; poor Fool: 2.1.276: (a) needy jester; (b, as 'poor fool':) poor dear.
'forehand: anticipatory.
forswear: solemnly deny; forsworn: proven a liar.
forward (adj.): 1.3.46: precocious.
frame (noun): 4.1.126: creativity; in frame of: in devising.
frame (vb.): create, compose.
from: 3.1.72: contrary to.

full: 1.1.92: completely.

gallop: false gallop: 3.4.80: (a) taught canter; (b) run of falsehood.

getting: begetting.

girdle: belt; turn his girdle: (probably) cope, adapt.

go: go about with: proceed deviously; go before: 4.2.18: (a) precede; (b) take precedence over; go to: 1.1.172, 4.2.75: go on, go away.

God's my life: God save my life.

good-den: i.e., 'God give you good even': good afternoon or good evening.

Goodman: Mr.

good-year: 'What the good-year': (probably) 'What the devil'.

gossip (noun): old chatterer.

got: 5.4.50: begot.

go to: 1.1.172, 4.2.75: go away, go on.

govern: regulate.

grace: (i: 1.3.18, 2.3.28:) favour; (ii: 2.3.27:) admirable quality.

gracious: attractive.

Great Cham: Great Ruler: e.g. Kublai Khan.

gross: coarse, vulgar.

guarded: decorated.

guerdon: recompense.

gull (noun): deception.

gull (vb.): trick.

habit: clothing.

haggard: wild female hawk.

hale (vb.): haul.

halting: limping.

hangman: 3.2.10: (a) executioner; (b) rogue.

hap (noun): accident.

happiness: dear happiness: great good fortune; good outward happiness: good external appearance.

hare-finder: man who locates a hare to be hunted.

harpy: legendary foul female monster.

head: to thy head: to thy face.

Headborough: parish constable.

heart-burned: afflicted with discomfort (e.g. 'acid indigestion') in the chest.

Hector: legendary Trojan warrior-hero.

Hercules: legendary hero who completed twelve arduous labours.

high-proof: powerfully.

hobby-horse: buffoon.

hold: hold friends: stay on good terms; hold it up: keep it up.

holp: helped.

holy thistle: *Cnicus benedictus*: plant with healing powers.

honest: 3.1.84: (probably) well-meant.

honesty: honour.

horn-mad: 1.1.233: (a) angry as a charging bull; (b) angry as a cuckolded husband.

hot-blood: eager young man.

how: 3.1.60: however.

huddling: heaping.

humour (noun): (i: 1.1.111, 2.3.220:) disposition; (ii: 3.2.24:) bodily fluid; (iii: 5.1.177:) mood.

humour (vb.): 2.1.334: (a) indulge, (b) influence, win over.

Hymen: classical god of marriage.

idea: **idea of her life**: her living image.

i'faith: truly.

ill-well: aptly as infirm.

important: importunate.

impose me: subject me.

impossible: 2.1.118, 214: incredible.

in a tale: telling the same lie.

incense (vb.): incite.

indeed: **a man indeed**: 5.1.89: (a) a man by action; (b) a true man.

infernal: hellish.

infinite of thought: utmost extent of thought.

instance: (i: 2.2.36:) evidence; (ii: 5.2.62:) maxim.

intelligence: information.

intend: pretend.

interjection: interruptive or parenthetical exclamation.

invention: inventiveness.

inward: hidden.

inwardness: intimate friendship.

Jack: rascal, bad lad.

jade: unruly horse; **a jade's trick**: (perhaps) dodging away.

jealousy: suspicion.

Jove: Jupiter, the supreme Roman deity.

just: (i: 2.1.23, 5.1.156:) just so, precisely; (ii: 2.1.314:) exact.

keep your way: carry on.

kid-fox: fox-cub.

kind: 1.1.23: natural; **kindly**: 4.1.73: natural.

kindness: 1.1.23: tenderness.

lanthorn: lantern.

lapwing: peewit.

large: sexually suggestive; **largely**: fully.

league: roughly 3 miles (4.8 km.).

learn: 4.1.29: teach.

leavy: leafy.

lechery: 3.3.152: (error for) treachery.

Leonato: 'Lion-born'.

level (vb.): aim.

lewd: 5.1.315: (a) low, base; (b) rascally.

liberal: 4.1.90: (a) loose-tongued; (b) licentious, coarse.

libertine: licentious person.

lief: gladly.

light (adj.): 3.4.33: (a) immoral, wanton; (b) light in weight.

'Light o' Love': title of a dance-song.

liked: **liked to have had**: nearly had.

limed: caught.

list (vb.): please.

liver: supposedly the source of passion.

lock: 3.3.155: love-lock: long dangling lock of hair.

lodge: 2.1.186: (a) hut; (b) form or burrow.

lute: stringed instrument.

luxurious: lecherous.

maid: virgin.

make: 3.3.49: do.

mannerly-modest: graciously-modulated.

March-chick: bird hatched early; hence, upstart.

mark (noun): sign; man at a mark: man who shows an archer where his arrow has fallen.

mark (vb.): regard, notice.

marl: clay.

marry (interjection, as at 1.3.40): by the Virgin Mary: indeed.

Mass: By the Holy Mass.

matter: 1.1.241, 2.1.291: sense.

means: 4.1.195: funds.

measure. (i. 1.3.2, 3.) moderation; (ii: 2.1.61: a) moderation; (b) a dance; (c) a particular stately dance; (iii: 2.1.63, 66:) stately dance.

med'cinable: medicinal, healing.

meet (adj.): appropriate; be meet with: get even with.

mercy: I cry you mercy: I beg your pardon.

merely: purely, utterly.

mettle: 2.1.51, 5.1.132: (a) material; (b) spirit.

milksop: spoilt weakling.

Millaine: Milan.

misgovernment: misconduct.

misprision: misjudgement, error.

misprizing: 2.1.52: (a) despising; (b) undervaluing.

mistrust (vb.): suspect.

misuse: (i: 2.1.209:) abuse; (ii: 2.2.24:) deceive.

model: builder's plan.

modest: modest office: respectable task.

moe: more in number. ('More' once meant 'greater in quantity'.)

monument: monumental tomb; live . . . in monument: live in memory.

moral (noun): 3.4.65: hidden meaning.

moral (adj.): 5.1.30: (a) moralising; (b) patient.

mortifying mischief: deadly affliction.

Mountanto: 1.1.26: (a) Aspiring; (b) Thruster.

moving-delicate: 4.1.226: (a) movingly graceful; (b) deliciously mobile.

mum: silence.

name: none of name: nobody noteworthy.

narrowly: closely.

naught: worthless; naughty: 4.2.64; 5.1.283: (a) worthless; (b) wicked.

night-gown: dressing-gown.

night-raven: nocturnal bird of ill-omen.

noble: 2.3.30: (a) of noble character; (b) resembling the 'noble', a gold coin.

noisome: disgusting.

nonce: **for the nonce**: for that one occasion.

'non-come': 3.5.56: (a) perhaps for '*non compos mentis*', unsound mind; (b) perhaps for 'non-plus', state of bewilderment.

nothing: **meant nothing to my sword**: had no plan to use my sword.

obey: 3.3.160: (error for) oblige.

odorous: 3.5.14: (error for) odious.

office: (i: 2.1.152, 5.1.27:) business; (ii: 3.1.12, 4.1.264, 5.4.14:) task; (iii: 3.5.47, 53:) position; **modest office**: respectable task.

old: 5.2.80: great.

once: 5.1.198: at any time; **'tis once**: 1.1.278: (a) it's once and for all; (b) in brief.

opinioned: 4.2.62: (error for) pinioned.

orb: 4.1.56: sphere (here, the moon).

organ of her life: living part of her body.

orthography: 2.3.19: i.e. ortho-grapher, but here meaning 'rhetorician' or 'stylist'.

ostentation: display.

out-facing: insolent.

packed: complicit.

paint: **paint himself**: use cosmetics on his face; **paint out**: depict fully.

palabras (from Spanish *pocas palabras*): words (i.e. 'few words are needed').

parrot-teacher: repetitive chatterer.

part: (i: 1.1.204:) argument; (ii: 1.1.281:) rôle.

passing (adv.): extremely.

patience: **wake your patience**: 5.1.102: (a) trouble your patience; (b) invoke your patience.

pennyworth: **fit...with a pennyworth**: give . . . more than he bargained for.

pent-house: overhanging part of a roof.

peradventure: perhaps.

perfumer: fumigator.

pestilence: plague.

Philemon: legendary old man whose humble cottage was visited by Jove.

Phoebus: Phoebus Apollo, the sun-god.

piety: 4.2.72: (error for) impiety.

pike: spike.

pipe: simple wind-instrument.

plaintiffs: 5.1.239: (error for) defendants.

pleachèd: with interwoven boughs and stems.

pluck up: collect yourself.

politic: crafty.

poniard: dagger.

possess: 5.1.267: inform;
possessed: 3.3.136–7, 142:
(a) informed, instructed;
(b) convinced; (c)
dominated as by a devil.

practise on: trick.

pray: **I pray thee**: please.

preceptial: in the form of
advice.

predestinate: inevitable.

present (vb.): 3.3.68:
represent.

presently: immediately.

press me to death: kill me
slowly by heaping weights
on me.

Prester John: legendary
Christian ruler of a remote
region.

prized: esteemed.

prohibit: 5.1.310: (error for)
permit.

prolong: postpone.

proof: 2.1.157: demonstration;
your own proof: testing for
yourself.

proper: (i: 2.3.169: a) handsome;
(b) worthy, (ii. 4.1.174:)
appropriate; **proper saying**:
likely story.

propose (noun): 3.1.12: (a)
conversation; (b) purpose.

proposing (vb.): conversing.

prospect: vision.

protest: (i: 4.1.276, 281, 284:)
declare; (ii: 5.1.144:) proclaim.

prove: 1.3.60: find out.

publish: proclaim.

purchase: 3.1.70: earn.

push: **made a push at**: 5.1.38:
(a) tried to repel; (b) said
'Pish!' to.

put down: 2.1.248–51: (a)
defeat; (b) copulate with.

quaint: 3.4.20: (a) ingenious;
(b) dainty.

qualify: reduce.

qualm: sudden nausea or
faintness.

queasy: squeamish; **queasy
stomach**: fastidious
disposition.

question: **in question**:
3.3.163: (a) in demand;
(b) subject to legal
proceedings; (c)
questionable, of doubtful
value.

quips: 2.3.219: (a) jests;
(b) retorts.

quirks: **odd quirks**: 2.3.215:
(a) occasional quips;
(b) peculiar turns.

quit me of: avenge myself on.

quondam: old-time.

rack (vb.): exaggerate.

ranges evenly with: matches,
suits.

rare: exceptional.

rearward: **on the rearward**:
in the wake.

reason: 5.1.197: (a) argument;
(b) raisin.

rebato: 3.4.6: (a) stiff
ornamented collar or ruff;
(b) support for a ruff (*O.E.D.*).

recheat: a hunting-horn call
to summon hounds.

reckoning: account to settle.
recover: 3.3.151–2: (error for) discover.
redemption: 4.2.52: (error for) damnation.
reechy: grimy, sooty.
reformed: 5.1.240: (error for) informed.
remembered: 1.1.11: rewarded.
reportingly: on the basis of hearsay.
reprove: disprove, refute.
reverence: 2.3.116: elderly respectability.
rheum: tears.
right (adj.): 3.3.151: worthy.
rod: bundle of thin twigs (e.g. birch).
sad: (i: 1.1.157, 1.3.49, 5.1.195:) serious; (ii: 1.3.2, 11, 2.1.253, 254, 257, 3.2.17, 5.4.120:) melancholy; **sadly**: 2.3.201: seriously.
Saint Peter: the gate-keeper of heaven.
salved: 1.1.275: (a) justified; (b) anointed with balm; hence, smoothed.
saving your reverence: 'with all due respect to you': an apology for mentioning something offensive.
scab: 3.3.92: (a) crust on graze or cut; (b) scoundrel.
scambling: quarrelsome.
scape: escape.
scorn...with my heels: kick out at, spurn.

Scotch jig: lively dance.
scruple: an apothecary's 20-grain weight.
seal (noun): 4.1.165: proof.
seal (vb.): 5.1.226: conclude.
season: 4.4.141: renewal.
second (vb.): assist.
sedges: reeds, water-grass.
seize upon: take possession of.
semblance: appearance.
senseless: 3.3.20: (error for) sensible.
sensible: 1.1.227: (a) sensitive; (b) rational.
sentence: moral maxim.
service: 1.1.41–4: (a) military service; (b) participation at meal-time.
seven-night: a just seven-night: a week exactly.
several: separate.
sexton: clergyman's assistant.
shift: for a shift: as a makeshift.
shrewd: shrewish, sharp.
sign: 4.1.32: mere appearance.
Signior, signior (Italian *signore*): Mr, gentleman.
simpleness: integrity, plain honesty.
sit you (colloquialism): 2.3.106: sit.
slops: baggy breeches.
smock: slip, simple frock.
smoking: fumigating.
soft and fair: slowly and clearly.
soft you: wait, hold on.
sort (noun): 1.1.6, 29: rank.
sort (vb.): turn out.

speed's: speed us: bless us.

spell him backward: completely
misrepresent him.

spit (noun): metal rod on which
roasting meat was rotated.

sport: in sport: joking.

squarer: 1.1.67: (a) quarrelsome person; (b) swaggerer.

squire: proper squire: smart
young suitor.

staff: lance-shaft.

stairs: keep below stairs: remain
a servant.

stale (noun): wanton woman;
common stale: public
prostitute; contaminated
stale: 2.1.22: (a) polluted
whore; (b) corrupted whore.

stamp (vb.): prove.

stand (vb.): 3.3.23, 25, 29: stop.

start-up: upstart.

state and ancientry: traditional
decorum.

stay: 3.3.69, 72, 74: stop.

stomach: appetite; queasy
stomach: fastidious disposition.

stood out: 1.3.17: rebelled.

stops (noun): 3.2.52: (a) denials;
(b) frets on a stringed instrument; (c) tuning-holes in a
wind-instrument.

strain: 2.1.332–3: (a) lineage;
(b) disposition; answer every
strain for strain: 5.1.12:
(a) correspond in every
emotion; (b) respond as in
musical antiphony.

strange face: inappropriate
guise.

study of imagination: reflective
scrutiny.

stuffed: (i: 1.1.47–9:
a) admirably replete;
(b) merely padded out;
(ii: 3.4.54–5: a) 'stuffed up',
having nose congested by a
cold; (b) pregnant.

subscribe for: take the part of,
deputise for; subscribe him:
declare him.

success: what follows.

suffer: 5.2.53–4: (a) experience;
(b) suffer from.

sufficiency: capability.

suffigance: (error for) sufficient.

suit: 2.1.64, 307: wooing,
courting; suited: 5.1.213:
(a) in accord; (b) dressed up;
suit with: match.

sun-burnt: marred by sun-tan.

sure: 1.3.56: reliable.

suspect: 4.2.68: (error for)
respect.

sworn brother: brother-in-
arms, pledged to aid his
comrade.

tabor: small drum.

tale: in a tale: telling the same
lie.

tartly: sourly.

tattling: chattering.

tax: (i: 1.1.39:) censure;
(ii: 2.3.42:) command.

temper (vb.): concoct.

temple: church.

temporize with the hours:
1.1.237: (a) defer the
inevitable; (b) waste time.

tend: 1.3.13: attend, wait.

tender: **make tender of**: offer.

tenure: tenor, purport.

terminations: 2.1.217–18:
(a) terms; (b) definitions.

thick-pleached alley: pathway
between densely intertwined
plants, bushes or trees.

throughly: thoroughly.

thwart: obstruct; **thwarting**:
3.2.115: frustrating.

time: **in good time**: 2.1.60:
(a) at the appropriate time;
(b) to a musical tempo.

tire (noun): head-dress with
false hair and ornaments.

to a lord: 1.1.46: compared to
a lord.

tongues: **hath the tongues**: is
a linguist.

tooth-picker: tooth-pick.

top: **by the top**: by the
forelock.

trace (vb.): pace.

travail: **on this travail**: from
this labour.

treatise: account.

trencher-man: man with keen
appetite.

trial: 2.2.35: proof; **trial of a
man**: 5.1.66: (a) single combat;
(b) a test of manhood.

trim (adj.): 4.1.315: smooth.

troth, **by my troth**: truly.

trow: 3.4.50: I wonder.

true: 3.3.58: honest.

truth: 2.2.42: proof.

try: judge.

tuition: protection.

tune: 3.4.37–9: (a) mood;
(b) tone; (c) melody.

twine: **smallest twine**:
weakest thread.

twist a story: spin a yarn.

unconfirmed: inexperienced.

undergo: be subject to.

undo: 5.4.20: (a) unbind;
(b) ruin.

unmeet: improper.

unseasonable: incongruous.

untowardly: unfavourably.

up and down: 2.1.99: (a)
exactly; (b) wavering.

use (noun): 2.1.245: interest.

utterèd: 5.3.20: (a) fully
expressed; (b) ousted,
driven out.

vagrom: (version of) vagrant.

vane: windvane.

varlet: 4.2.66: (a) rascal;
(b) menial.

Venice: Italian city noted for
its courtesans.

Venus: Roman deity of love.

Verges: surname from
'verjuice', the sour juice
of unripe fruit.

vex: torment.

victual: food.

vigitant: (version of) vigilant.

vild: vile; **vildly**: vilely.

villainy: 2.1.120: gross slanders.

visor: mask or half-mask.

vouchsafe: permit.

Vulcan: the blacksmith of the
gods.

wag: 5.1.16: (perhaps) play the
fool.

wait upon: 1.3.61, 3.5.50: attend.

walk a bout: join the circuit of a dance.

warrant (noun): evidence.

warrant (vb.): assure, assure you.

warren: 2.1.186: (a) enclosed area for breeding game; (b) abode of hares or rabbits.

watching: staying awake.

weeds: garments.

weight: matter of weight: important matter.

well-favoured: handsome.

wide: 4.1.61: wide of the mark: falsely.

willow garland: emblem of a forsaken lover.

windy: windward.

'Win me and wear me!': 'Until you defeat me, I am no trophy!'

wise gentleman: 5.1.158: (ironic for) old fool.

wit: intelligence; **beside their wit**: distracted, deranged; **wit-cracker**: witty mocker; **wits: five wits**: five mental faculties; **witty**: clever.

withal: (i: 1.2.19:) with it; (ii: 2.3.234:) with.

wonderful: amazing.

wont: accustomed.

woodbine: honeysuckle.

woollen: in the woollen: between blankets, without sheets.

word: at a word: in short.

world: goes . . . to the world: gets married; **world to see**: strange world to behold.

wrest: pervert.

wring: writhe.

write against: publish a denunciation of.